THE
PATH TO
POSITIVITY

THE
PATH TO
POSITIVITY

Proven Positive Thinking Techniques
for Getting Motivated and Living Your Best Life

CAITLIN MARGARET

R
ROCKRIDGE
PRESS

Interior and Cover Designer: Peatra Jariya
Art Producer: Sue Bischofberger
Editor: Nora Spiegel
Production Editor: Chris Gage

ISBN: Print 978-1-64152-619-7 | eBook 978-1-64152-620-3

R0

To my partner
in marriage and mischief,
Abhinav. Thank you for
believing in all my dreams and
for teaching me how deep my
laughter could go. You are
the wind beneath
my wild wings.

CONTENTS

. . . Harness positive thinking, measuring your progress along the way, and change your life —and your world— forever.

INTRODUCTION

Many of us feel the urgency to change our world for the better. We want to make a difference and to create the solutions that are most needed right now. And yet, these changes can often feel out of our grasp. But how we begin to change our world depends, first, on our own ability to change and address the needs in our own lives. Without establishing a foundation within ourselves upon which to effect change in others, our efforts can seem disconnected and lack the results we long for.

Change within ourselves can take countless forms. How do we know where to start? This is where positivity comes in. The ability to frame our experiences through a lens of positivity gives us the ability to reshape our inner world and the tools for living our best lives. Perhaps you've dabbled in positive thinking before but you couldn't make it stick or it didn't get the results you wanted. As someone who struggled with depression and anxiety for over a decade, I get it. No matter how many affirmations I read every night, as soon as I received a stressful assignment, or I bumped into my ex, I'd fall headfirst back into negativity.

I realized that I needed more than inspiring anecdotes. I needed a proven path to positivity. I completed my master's degree in social work from Columbia University, where I learned

cutting-edge positive thinking techniques in modern psychology. I then taught coping skills to people with severe and persistent mental illness, worked with children impacted by armed conflict, and eventually started two social enterprises in India that focused on rural, marginalized populations. During my time in India, I learned the value of stillness and mindfulness, as well as the art of surrendering to uncertainty, failure, and imperfection. Combining the best of both worlds, I healed my mental health, improved my mood, and reactivated my motivation.

Positive thinking then empowered me to level up in every area of my life. I felt more confident at work, so I co-created multiple companies and nonprofits around the world. I felt more positive about the people in my life, so my relationships flourished. And I felt worthy and capable of building a balanced, healthy life, so I did (and do) . . . in spite of the stressors of the modern world.

Today, the information and practices I used to build a positive mind-set are at the foundation of my life coaching practice, Radiant Wholeness. And in this book, I am sharing them with you. You'll begin by understanding what positive thinking is, and what it's not. With this understanding, you'll assess your current positivity level and set concrete goals about how you'll leverage positive thinking to improve your life. Then we'll head to the inner gym, where I'll train you to build new mind-set muscles. You'll learn how to overcome stress and conquer your brain's negativity bias. You'll also gain insight into the three components of every experience you can always control in order to create a more positive outcome.

Next, you'll learn how to design your life in a way that naturally creates positive experiences every day. You'll define your unique values, understand how to live them, and practice concrete strategies to avoid the comparison trap and to live from self-acceptance. From this strong foundation, you'll be trained on how to use your positive mind-set to get unstuck and achieve your goals. You'll master high-level skills to stay positive in the face of uncertainty, let go of perfectionism, and maintain motivation to keep kicking ass. Finally, you'll ensure your long-term success. You'll learn strategies for self-care and how to use mindfulness, self-compassion, and boundary setting to sustain positive thinking. You'll understand how to consistently become your best self, and how to enjoy the journey, even when it seems like the world around you is falling apart.

This path to positivity is inspiring, but it's also practical. Every technique I share with you is backed by research, and every chapter builds on the knowledge and skills established in the previous one. You'll harness positive thinking, measuring your progress along the way and changing your life—and your world—forever.

"Progress is impossible
without change, and those
who cannot change their
minds cannot change
anything."

—GEORGE BERNARD SHAW

CHAPTER ONE

Establishing Your Positive Mental Attitude

Since the days of Aristotle, humans have striven for healthy minds, ones that focuses on positive qualities, like strength, hope, optimism, courage, and the capacity for meaningful insight. But many of us still struggle to maintain positivity on a daily basis. There are two main reasons for this: first, a misunderstanding of what positive thinking entails, and second, a lack of a systematic approach. Ideas are easier to sell when they're simple, so as the positive thinking movement has become more mainstream, many have glossed over the deep, and at times difficult, inner work required to create and maintain a positive mindset. This includes acknowledging the important place that negative thoughts and experiences hold in creating a positive life. Positive thinking is a skill that can be mastered, like gardening or learning a new language. But it takes commitment and a plan. You need to show up every day and attend to the workings of your inner world, where you learn the basics and then graduate into increasingly complex skills and applications.

This chapter will prepare you for a much more substantive and sustainable journey to positivity than you've experienced before. You'll gain a new understanding of what positive thinking entails and learn about the latest research showing how positivity enables transformation in your well-being, career, and relationships. You'll also create personalized goals for how you will apply the positive thinking skills in this book to improve your own life, so that you have concrete ways to measure the success of the work you're putting in.

HOW DID YOU GET HERE?

How many times have you tried to become "a more positive person" but found yourself back in the same rut, repeating the same negativity you promised to give up? Well, you're not alone! Most people struggle to make lasting positive changes in their lives. Only 8 percent of people, for example, actually stick to their New Year's resolution. That's because making change involves ambiguity, and the brain tries to avoid ambiguity at all costs because it means it has to work harder to account for different possible outcomes. Instead, the brain loves experiences it's familiar with, including the negative thoughts you're used to thinking, and it shuns anything "new," like positive perspectives you're trying to adopt, because it takes more cognitive effort to incorporate them. But the brain doesn't do this because it simply doesn't like change. It does this because it's trying to maximize its own efficiency, and it can be pretty inefficient to acquire new information. But with a little coaxing, and a little encouragement, your brain *can* adapt and help you make lasting changes in behavior.

For example, you might want to develop a positive body image, but unless you're already accustomed to practicing acceptance with your body's imperfections, your brain will not easily support this goal without some additional training. Its aversion to ambiguity means it will reject the vulnerable, unpracticed experience of positive self-talk in the mirror and try to get you to stop doing it by sending out all kinds of ready and well-worn negative thoughts and emotions, like "this won't work," or "start tomorrow, not today." But there are many things that you can do to overcome your brain's bias against ambiguity in order to sustain positive changes. The first step is to get clear on *why* you're doing this work.

Why did you pick up this book? In general, I've seen four primary reasons, or some combination therein, people strive to think more positively. People want to (1) get motivated, (2) climb out from under bad feelings, (3) let go of stress, or (4) live a better life.

Seeking Motivation

There's nothing worse than having big dreams but no energy or desire to pursue them on a day-to-day basis. Negative thinking is often responsible for this lack of drive: If you're always thinking about how difficult your day will be, or worrying about how you'll mess things up, then, let's face it, staying in bed and watching Netflix is going to feel better than going after your dreams. In other words, accomplishing your goals can be difficult when you're mired in negative thinking and don't have the motivation to get started or pick up where you left off. But positive thinking breaks the cycle of negativity and can be the boost you need to get moving. It also reminds you that you're courageous and competent enough to make small steps toward your goals every day. When your mind is expecting good things to come of your efforts, like a promotion, a delicious meal, or a fun date, it gets your blood pumping and your enthusiasm flowing and you feel naturally motivated to take action.

Feeling Depressed

If you're feeling depressed, life can be inordinately dark and difficult, and it can be hard to do much of anything, let alone feel positively about yourself or your circumstances. Research from the *Scandinavian Journal of Psychology* shows that negative interpretations of experiences leads to negative views of yourself and the world, and that people who have more negative automatic thoughts are vulnerable to depression. This is why positive thinking is such a powerful intervention for improving your mood and overcoming depression.

In fact, according to research cited in *Clinical Practice & Epidemiology in Mental Health*, positive thinking improves depression by increasing positive emotions and helping people compassionately cope with their negative emotions.

Letting Go of Stress

Another reason you might be drawn to positive thinking is because of its stress-busting effects. In the modern world, it's impossible to avoid computer crashes, flat tires, canceled flights, difficult relationships, or life transitions. These experiences can trigger stressful psychological and physiological symptoms, such as emotional overwhelm and disconnection, or somatic issues, like sweaty palms, chest pain, and digestive issues, all of which add to the challenging circumstances.

Research shows, however, that it's not these symptoms themselves but how we react to them that determines our level of stress. In their book *Stress, Appraisal, and Coping,* psychologists Richard Lazarus and Susan Folkman compile two decades of research, demonstrating that how we perceive a stressful life event—as threatening, neutral-positive, or not relevant—is different from person to person and contributes to the huge individual differences we have in coping with these experiences.

When your flight gets canceled, positive thinking skills help you reframe your experience, keeping in mind what you're grateful for, how you'll cope, and how you've overcome similar circumstances in the past. Whether it's your career, your commute, or your overactive kid that is causing you angst, cultivating positive emotions like joy and playfulness significantly reduces your stress.

Looking for Something Better

Last, maybe you're looking to build a meaningful career, loving relationships, authentic friendships, a healthy lifestyle, or financial security. Whatever it is, chances are good you're probably craving something more out of your life. A 2018 study by Cigna showed that 43 percent of Americans feel that their relationships are not meaningful and that they are isolated from others. Another study, by Ipsos, in the same year indicated that a whopping 80 percent are dissatisfied with their bodies. Furthermore, research association The Conference Board reports that only 51 percent of Americans are satisfied with their jobs.

Fortunately, vast numbers of studies show that positive thinking is correlated with greater success in many areas of our lives, including our relationships, careers, and self-image. However, it is that you want to level up, positive and self-affirming thoughts bolster your feelings of self-worth, make you more likely to expect positive outcomes, and, consequently, more likely to pursue your goals. When the going gets rough, positive thinking makes you more resilient by helping you focus on finding solutions.

DO THIS NOW: WHAT ARE YOU LOOKING FOR?

You may not know where this book is taking you (yet), or you may feel uncomfortable with some of the challenging exercises I provide in the coming chapters. Because of the brain's tendency to avoid ambiguity, you'll be tempted to toss this book aside and thwart your progress on the path to positivity. But if you're clear on why positivity matters to you, you'll be much more likely to stay the course and get the results you desire.

Take a moment to clarify your "why." It's important that you write down your answers, not just move through them as a mental exercise. This will slow down your thoughts, as well as make you remember your reflection much better. I recommend that you use a special notebook or journal, dedicated exclusively to your path to positivity. This is the first of many exercises in which you'll be invited to be more introspective, and it's helpful to keep all your thoughts and insights in one place so you can refer back to them when you need them and document your progress over time.

Start by answering the following questions:

- What made you pick up this book? What were you thinking when you decided to purchase it?
- How do you think your life might change for the better when you regularly practice positive thinking?
- How might you benefit from using positive skills to get motivated, work through depression, and beat stress?
- Who do you know who is already a positive thinker, and what do you admire about them or value about being in their company?
- What skills, specifically, are you seeking to cultivate?
- How do you want to be, feel, or change by the end of this book?

Once you've answered all the questions, summarize your insights into one strong "why" statement.

"Why" statement: "I am committed to the path to positivity because . . . "

Remember, this "why" statement is critical to maintaining your progress. Whenever the path to positivity becomes challenging and you need to regain some perspective into your positive thinking practice, the first step is always to return here and revisit your "why."

WHAT'S POSITIVE THINKING, ANYWAY?

Some people equate positive thinking with incessant optimism. Others believe it's a type of avoidance, whereby unpleasant thoughts and situations are denied and suppressed until they go away. These definitions are not only inaccurate, but they also give positive thinking a bad reputation because they dismiss the negativity embedded in every human experience. We find a much better definition from researcher Barbara Fredrickson, who describes positivity as deep experiences of love, joy, amusement, gratitude, and hope that are accompanied by optimistic attitudes, meaning, and the "open mind, tender heart, relaxed limbs, and soft faces they usher in." Fredrickson's studies show that positive experiences help you build resources, such as resilience and meaningful relationships, that last much longer than a smile.

For practical purposes, this book will define positive thinking as a way of perceiving yourself and your situation that makes you feel confident and cared for. Let's dig deeper into the core components of positive thinking and how they contribute to your well-being.

Changing Your Frame of Mind

Is being rejected from a job a sign that you're incompetent or just a natural part of life? Is going to the gym an annoying chore or an act of self-care? It all depends on your frame of mind. Moreover, because the way you choose to think about these experiences impacts how you feel and how you behave going forward, positive thinking invites you to choose a perspective that will empower you to continue pursuing your goals. When you get rejected from a job, thinking you're a loser or that life's not fair makes you feel angry and lowers your confidence, which decreases your motivation in the job search. Positive thinking changes that frame of mind so that you learn from the experience and continue your search with optimism.

> Positive Thinking Rule #1:
> Adopt a helpful and hopeful perspective.

Challenging and Restructuring Your Thoughts

As previously discussed, negative thoughts are an easy way for the brain to manage ambiguity because negativity, especially if you're prone to negative thinking, uses less mental energy. But recognizing, challenging, and restructuring the negative thoughts, although more mentally tiring and vigorous, is the way to make important changes in your thinking.

When you recognize a negative thought, ask yourself if this thought is really true. For example, if you're feeling socially anxious on your way to a friend's party, it might be that you're conjuring up negative thoughts about the anticipated experience, and you tell yourself, "I'm terrible at making conversation with strangers." Positive thinking instructs you to challenge that negative thought by asking yourself, "Is this really true? Are there times when I'm good at making conversation? What's one thing people enjoy talking about with me?" This is known as an "exception question"—what are the exceptions to your negative thoughts, the times when the negative thought wasn't true?

When you challenge your negative thoughts, you develop a more realistic perspective about your situation. And simply saying the thought to yourself or, better, writing it down on paper will really help it sink in. Then you can restructure your thoughts to help yourself feel more confident, like: "I usually find one person that I connect with about music, so I'm hopeful that will happen today, too."

> Positive Thinking Rule #2:
> Challenge the truthfulness of your negative thoughts
> and restructure them to empower you.

Don't Talk About Yourself Like That!

My client Kristie's daughter got sick and was hospitalized for two weeks. Kristie was blaming and shaming herself, thinking: "What did I do wrong? Why did I become a mother? I'm clearly not up to this task. I'm screwing up this child."

This is a great example of negative self-talk. I asked Kristie how she would talk to her best friend if she was in this situation, and she said, "I'd tell her that I'm sorry she's going through this scary situation, that every mother makes a million mistakes, and that I know she'll get through it." Then I invited Kristie to talk to herself in this same compassionate tone—that's positive self-talk. Often, you are your own harshest critic. Positive thinking uses self-talk to focus on your strengths and compassionately address your weaknesses.

> Positive Thinking Rule #3:
> Talk to yourself the way you would talk to your best friend.

It's Okay to Be Unhappy

Simply put, it's not only unrealistic to avoid unhappiness, it's completely unhelpful. And oftentimes, the more you try to avoid something, the harder it becomes to ignore. Therefore, if you're constantly arguing with your spouse, or if you're feeling unappreciated by your critical boss, you need to give these negative emotional experiences extra care and attention. Don't gloss over them or pretend everything is fine. Often, negative feelings emerge when one of your core needs are unmet, such as safety, love, or rest. Positive thinking stops you from judging yourself or the other person and steers your mind to problem-solving, asking, "What do I need to navigate this situation more skillfully?" or "How can I support myself through this challenging experience?"

Positive Thinking Rule #4:
Approach your negative emotions with
curiosity, bravery, and kindness.

DO THIS NOW: ASSESS YOUR POSITIVITY

Positivity involves making a commitment to see the good in yourself and others, take responsibility for your well-being, and sit face-to-face with negativity, uncertainty, and discomfort. You're going to learn how to use positive thinking to fulfill all these commitments throughout this book, but it's great to take stock of where you are right now on the path to positivity.

Please score each item from 1 to 10, based on how true each statement is for you, with 1 being the lowest score and 10 being the highest. Then calculate your positivity score by adding your responses together.

1. I like myself, appreciate my strengths, and accept my imperfections.
2. My daily life and goals are very fulfilling because they are aligned with my core values.
3. I take responsibility for my relationship to my experiences by working with my thoughts, emotions, and behaviors.
4. I turn positive experiences into long-term resources. When good things happen, I proactively take time to appreciate, nourish, enrich, and share these experiences.

5. I surround myself with people who believe in kindness, gratitude, and positivity, and I cultivate deep, meaningful relationships with these people.
6. When I experience negative emotions, I pause before reacting and meet my thoughts and feelings with curiosity, compassion, and self-care.
7. I never avoid discomfort or uncertainty; I know I am resilient enough to overcome whatever circumstances I encounter.
8. When I feel lost or confused, I tap into the intuitive intelligence of my personal wisdom and honor its guidance.
9. When I fail, I always look for the growth and learning in my experience, and then continue to move forward toward my goals.
10. On a day-to-day basis, I expect good things, and I feel optimistic about my life.

My positivity score: _____ /100%

I know that this score looks like a grade you'd get after a test in high school, but positivity is not a pass-fail experience. Treat this assessment as a simple signpost, showing you where your positivity strengths are and where you'll benefit the most from learning new skills—and your first opportunity to put positive thinking into practice.

In the areas in which you didn't get a desirable score, can you talk to yourself like you would to your best friend, with an encouraging tone? Can you practice hopefulness about your ability to improve in these areas? Can you approach any negative emotions you're feeling with curiosity and kindness, asking how you can support yourself to bear this disappointment and improve in the future? As you progress through this book, you'll receive a lot more insight and tools about how to cultivate these positive perspectives, but for now just do the best you can.

WHAT POSITIVE THINKING IS NOT

Some people are skeptical about positive thinking because they see it as a Pollyannaish whitewashing of "real" life rather than an evidence-based tool to make the most of all the circumstances life serves up. Let's dispel the major positive thinking misconceptions.

Positive thinking is not "fake it till you make it." If you're having a hard day, there's no need to fake a smile. You just try not to get sucked into self-pity because that won't help you feel better. Positive thinking keeps you focused on self-care and solutions.

Positive thinking is not ignoring reality. If your goal is to make $150,000 in 2020, and you've only made $25,000 by November, you don't have to force yourself to believe you'll hit $100,000. Positive thinking reminds you that you had a lot of wins along the way and helps you learn from your shortcomings so you can constructively move forward.

Positive thinking is not a one-time exercise. You can't think, "I choose to love myself, inside out" one time and expect to never have another self-critical thought. Positive thinking is a practice.

Positive thinking is not a substitute for positive action. If your goal is to lose 20 pounds, positive thinking will help you feel motivated. But you still have to go to the gym.

WHY BOTHER?

For many of us, thinking negative thoughts is like breathing air—it's easy, automatic, and makes us feel in control. Your brain hates ambiguity, you'll recall, so it uses negative thoughts like worrying, judging yourself, and complaining about your life to create a temporary experience of comfort, making you feel prepared for the inevitable disappointments that await. And as much as your brain dislikes ambiguity, it loves familiarity. Maybe you're hooked on complaining to whoever will listen about your day's grievances: the dead-end job going nowhere, the coworker who won't mind their own business, or the underfunded public transit. This negative thinking feels comforting because it's so familiar.

Moreover, when you've been struggling for a long time to feel good about yourself or make progress toward your goals, positive thinking can feel like a ridiculous leap of faith. Going from "I'm not going to get any better at this" to "I'll give it another try" requires tremendous courage because you may, in fact, fail again.

So, if negativity is easier and often more comforting than positivity, why go through all this effort to train your brain to think differently? Well, imagine if you heard about a new medicine that not only keeps your immune system strong but also makes you experience more joy, gives you more energy, and helps you enjoy the people and circumstances around you more. You'd be heading straight to your local pharmacy, right?

Positive thinking has been scientifically proven to have all of these benefits, and it's the best supplement I know for living a fulfilling, successful life of physical and mental wellness. And this isn't a pill, so no prescription is required.

Better Overall Mental Health

As we discussed earlier, positive thinking can help you de-stress, overcome depression, and increase your motivation. Furthermore, research demonstrates that people who have a positive mind-set, those who have confidence in themselves and perceive the world positively, are more resilient in challenging times and are more motivated to bounce back from failure. A 2011 study in the *Journal of Counseling Psychology* showed that college students who had more positive "cognitions" (thoughts) reported significantly higher levels of life satisfaction, lower levels of depression, and higher levels of resilience.

Positive thinking interventions in mental health consistently show positive results, too. One 2015 study, for example, published in *Clinical Psychological Science*, showed that when people who struggle with anxiety were taught to think about worry in more positive ways, their intrusive thoughts lessened and their anxiety improved.

Better Physical Health Outcomes

Positivity isn't just medicine for your mind; it offers significant benefits for your physical health, too. A 2016 article in the *American Journal of Lifestyle Medicine* shows that positive thinking strengthens your immune system, decreases your blood pressure, and increases your tolerance for pain. Individuals with a positive attitude are less likely than their negative counterparts to experience a heart attack or catch a cold. And positive thinkers, as a whole, gain an average of eight years in their life spans—more time to enjoy their lives and follow their dreams.

Even when you do get sick, positive thinking helps you heal. For example, a 2014 study from the University of California, San Francisco demonstrated that HIV patients who practice positive thinking not only carry a lower level of the virus but are also more likely to take their medication correctly and less likely to need antidepressants to cope.

Strive More, Achieve More

When scientists studied academic achievement in college, what do you think was the most important factor for getting good grades? Intelligence, personality, previous academic achievement? Nope. Their findings, published in 2010 in the *Journal of Research in Personality*, indicate that the strongest indicator of academic achievement is hopeful, positive thinking. The students who expected positive outcomes as a result of their planning and efforts did, in fact, get the best outcomes.

Positivity empowers you to achieve more after graduation, too. From work performance to sales figures to income levels, numerous studies show that positive people strive and achieve more than their negative counterparts. Nice guys may finish last, but positive ones are thriving in our society.

Improve and Sustain Relationships

Positive thinking is also an elixir for relationships. Optimists, for example, feel more satisfied in their relationships. A 2006 study of dating couples published in the *Journal of Personality and Social Psychology* found that positive thinkers are more likely to interpret their partner's behaviors and intentions in positive ways, and they're more cognizant of how their relationship (even with its ups and downs) facilitates their personal goals and growth. The partners of optimists also report greater relationship satisfaction, indicating that the benefits of optimism are not just "in the head" of the optimists.

The same study also showed that positivity makes us better at managing conflict in our relationships, romantic and otherwise. Positive thinkers and their partners, for example, see each other as engaging more constructively during conflict, which in turn leads both people to feel that the conflict is better resolved.

Unsurprisingly, in a one-year follow-up, optimists were more likely to still be in their relationship.

DO THIS NOW: SET YOUR GOALS

As you can see, positive thinking helps you create positive change in your mental health, your physical wellness, your relationships, and your professional success. It's a practical tool that enables well-being and flourishing in so many areas of your life. However, as you make your way through this book (for the first time, anyway), I'd like you to choose one specific area of your life that you will try to transform through positive thinking.

I started learning Hindi a year before I got married because I wanted to be able to communicate with the 600 guests in my Indian wedding. With limited time on our hands, my teacher and I developed a brilliant plan: We focused exclusively on practicing the kinds of conversations I would have with my in-laws and wedding guests (rather than how to order dinner in a restaurant or ask a stranger for directions). This approach was a smashing success because I was clear on why I was learning Hindi and how to focus my efforts. I was able to hold a coherent conversation with every attendee! This increased my confidence in my language skills, which encouraged me to continue learning Hindi for other contexts as well.

Similarly, when you choose one specific area of your life upon which to apply your positive thinking skills, it empowers you to stay focused and clearly measure the impact of what you're learning in this book. Positivity will inevitably spill out into other areas of your life, but to best support your progress, start with one clear, focused goal for your positive thinking practice.

Start brainstorming what goal you would like to set by journaling the answers to the following questions:

1. Suppose tonight, while you sleep, a miracle occurs, and you wake up tomorrow to a life that you absolutely love. What's changed? Include specific details about what your relationships look like and feel like, as well as your health, your career, your lifestyle, your self-image, etc.

2. Out of all the changes you described in question one, which one is most important to you right now? Which transformation would create the most positive change in your overall well-being? For the sake of this exercise, we'll call this your "milestone."

3. Turn your milestone into a realistic and motivating action item that you can feasibly accomplish in the next three to six months. This may involve breaking down a bigger life goal into smaller milestones. For example, rather than "make new friends," you might write "meet three new people with shared interests."

When thinking about creating goals for yourself, it can be useful to develop SMART goals. The SMART acronym breaks a goal down into five distinct categories that help define the goal and create a template for how to achieve it:

Specific—Make sure the goal is specific and not overly broad (e.g., "I want to cook dinner at home more in order to save money.").

Measurable—You should be able to measure your progress (e.g., "I want to cook four dinners a week at home.").

Achievable—The goal should be within your reach. Don't make it overly ambitious and thereby hard to accomplish (e.g., "I am home four or five evenings per week. Therefore, cooking at home four nights a week is possible.").

Relevant—The goal should be applicable to your life and make sense in your current situation (e.g., "I would like to cook dinner at home four nights a week because I want to save money and lose weight. When I eat at home, it is often cheaper and healthier than eating out.").

Time-bound—The goal should not be indefinite. Instead, it should be for a limited time so that it can be actually completed (e.g., "I want to cook dinner at home four nights a week for the next month.").

Try formulating a goal of your choosing and then complete the following sentence in your journal, filling in the blanks. Notice that we are making this goal as tangible and measurable as possible so that it's easy to evaluate your progress and stay focused on the path to positivity.

My goal is to use positive thinking skills to _____ (milestone)_____ by _____(date)_____. I will measure my progress every week by ___ (quantifiable indicator of progress)_____.

Here are a couple examples:

My goal is to use positive thinking skills to increase my self-esteem by April 1, 2020. I will measure my progress every week using the Rosenberg Self-Esteem Scale.

My goal is to use positive thinking skills to be more honest with my husband by November 15, 2020. I will measure my progress every week by the number of times I lie to him or withhold my true feelings.

MAKING CHANGE

To create sustainable transformation, you need two things: the will and the way.

You already started cultivating "the will" by defining why you're here and what your goals are. As we commence on this journey, you'll be asked to practice positive thinking skills, like forgiving someone who wronged you or facing your most paralyzing fears. You will not always feel like doing these exercises because, despite how they help you grow in the long term, they create discomfort in the short term. However, if you keep returning to your goals and the reason you picked up this book, you'll increase your will to weather these challenges.

The other aspect of sustainable progress is "the way": knowing exactly what steps to take and how to take them in order to reach your goals. I'll be divulging these details in the coming chapters, but before we dive in, I want to give you three attitudinal foundations to maximize your results.

Keep It Current

The most common method of sabotaging success in the future is getting stuck in the past. My client Dan had started—and quit—at least 15 different diets before we met. Dan asked me to be his "accountability coach," checking in with him three times a day about his meals so that he'd feel pressure to stay on track. I wouldn't oblige, though, because I knew that the moment we stopped working together, he'd go back to his old ways. In the long term, the only accountability coach you'll ever listen to is the one in your head. Dan needed to forgive himself for his past and learn what kind of negative thoughts and emotions were influencing him to eat in ways that were out of sync with his goals. He also needed to understand how to be compassionate with himself so when he did slip up, he wouldn't beat himself up and abandon his mission, but rather learn from his mistakes and refocus on his goal. These positive thinking skills empowered Dan to finally stay in control of his mind and maintain his new dietary protocols.

Similarly, no matter what your change-making track record looks like, approach the goals you set in this book as a clean slate. According to a 2019 article by Harvard Health Publishing, the least effective strategies for long-lasting behavior change are those hinged on fear or regret, whereas the most successful changes are self-motivated and rooted in positive thinking. Your success, therefore, hinges on keeping your mind on your future goals and trusting the evidence-based tools I provide in this book to recalibrate your mind for success.

Take on the Challenge

So, you've chosen to let go of the past, but what if you slip up in the present? Let's say you set the goal of applying positive thinking to improving your relationship with your mother. Then she calls you up, nags for 20 minutes, and *bam!* you're consumed by negative thoughts about her and you hang up the phone.

How should you handle this perceived failure? First, acknowledge it with honesty and accept responsibility for your experience. Second, remember that nobody has ever created anything meaningful without substantial discomfort, failure, and revision. In fact, every single model of behavior change includes failure as part of the process, so messing up and realizing that you're doing it is a sign that you're in the process of making changes. Finally, choose to see this challenge as an opportunity to do better the next time. Ask yourself, "What feedback can I take from this failure? What needs more attention the next time I try this?"

Don't Lose Focus (But It's Okay If You Do)

Creating positivity is like baking bread. You mix together all the ingredients, place them in an oven, and let the dough rise. The tools I'm giving you in this book are your ingredients, but they will only consolidate into powerful habits if you bake them in the heat of your intense focus and commitment. This path is all about practice. I will give you the skills and the directions, but you have to apply them every day in order to create meaningful results. So, decide right now that this is your priority for the next three months and commit to practicing the skills you're learning here at least once a day. Journal about your insights and progress daily and download an app to remind you to practice what you're learning. Remember that you will fail at some point and that there will be days you'll feel distracted or disheartened. That is always a part of growth, so as soon as you recognize it, simply return to your commitment and reset your sights forward toward your goals.

YOUR PATH TO POSITIVITY

We're about to embark on the most empowering, inspiring, and transformative journey of your life. Like any journey, it's always nice to know your itinerary ahead of time, so here's a preview of the miraculous vistas and delectable dishes you'll experience on this adventure.

Your Brain on Positivity

In chapter 2, you'll learn about the connection between your thoughts, your feelings, and your actions, and you'll understand how to take responsibility for your experiences by consciously crafting these three elements. You'll get insight on cutting-edge research on neuroplasticity (aka the science of changing your brain) and understand why habits are the key to successful transformation. Then you'll acquire techniques to overcome your negative thoughts, practicing various tools for letting go of the past and dealing with disappointment, guilt, and shame. This is challenging work, but the rewards are so sweet. You'll feel lighter and more capable of handling adversity, and most important, you'll have newfound space in your mind for emerging positive thoughts to settle in.

Finally, you'll learn how to cultivate and savor these positive thoughts and emotions. The daily experiences of joy, hopefulness, curiosity, and appreciation will not only help you feel better, but they will also nurture the health, wisdom, and community that will help you fulfill your long-term goals.

Living Your Values

In chapter 3, we move beyond your momentary thoughts and emotions to look at your life as a whole. In any circumstance, you can proactively cultivate positivity by working with your thoughts, your feelings, and your actions, but you can also go the other way around by designing a life that is so fulfilling and so enjoyable that it serves as a wellspring for frequent positive experiences.

You'll get clear on your personal values and use these insights to design what I call "goals with soul," or changes in your relationships, career, and lifestyle that will make you feel a sense of purpose and connection each day. Then, anchored in the security and importance of your values, you'll learn how to push past discomfort, overcome the comparison trap, and forgive yourself for your mistakes.

Taking Action

Of course, even when you are living in alignment with your values, you'll still face challenges on the way to your goals. You'll slip up, forget your daily practice, or get a promotion you don't feel qualified to take. You'll put a bid on your dream house, only to have it get rejected, or you'll date one person for months without knowing if they're "the one." This is where most people lose their motivation, pack their bags, and go home to status quo and negative ways of thinking. But not you, my courageous reader.

In chapter 4, you'll learn the positive thinking skills that will keep you motivated and moving forward. You'll learn how to deal with imperfection, confront your fears, open yourself up to uncertainty, and overcome procrastination. You'll also activate your Wise Mind, which is the intuitive wisdom that can help you navigate difficult decisions and overwhelming circumstances. I'll even share some information about the most up-to-date research on effective goal setting and progress tracking.

Nurturing Positivity

By the time you reach chapter 5, you'll understand how to activate positivity by working with your thoughts, feelings, and actions as well as how to cultivate meaning and fulfillment through a values-led life. This final section will provide you with the strategies for maintaining and enhancing these positivity achievements so that you can stay on the path even after you close this book for the final time.

You'll learn how to say no and set boundaries with the people and situations that drain your energy and discourage your positivity. Even more important, you'll cultivate positive relationships built on the foundation of kindness and gratitude. These relationships will nourish your positivity practice and provide the support you require when times get tough. Finally, you'll create rituals of mindfulness, self-care, and compassion to recharge your positivity when your energy is running low, and you will raise your self-esteem to meet the challenges along your life's journey. You'll walk away with confidence and capabilities to live your best life.

POSITIVITY IN PRACTICE

You've now set the foundation for your positive transformation. You know what positive thinking entails, how it will benefit your life, and how, specifically, you'll apply the tools you're learning in this book to improve your life and well-being.

Feeling excited? Maybe a little nervous? Unsure? Don't worry! I'm here with you the whole time. Now, let's try to put into practice one of the critical aspects of positive thinking that we discussed in this chapter: positive expectations.

1. Write down what you're expecting will happen to you as you begin practicing positive thinking skills in the context of your goals. Make a list of the first three things that come into your mind. Don't force yourself to have positive expectations. Just write down whatever comes to mind.

2. Now review the three expectations you wrote down. Are your expectations positive, negative, or skeptical?

3. Get curious about your negative and skeptical expectations. No judgment here: Just be inquisitive about how your mind works.

    How do these negative expectations make you feel? Are they helpful to you?

    Are these negative expectations a result of your past experiences? Are you willing to let them go in order to move forward?

    Are these negative expectations based on negative perceptions of yourself and your capacity to change? Would your best friend also think this about you, or would they have a more uplifting expectation you could borrow?

What experience can you remember and draw from to challenge your negative expectations? What evidence is there that you can be more hopeful here?

Even if your negative expectations do unfold, can you remember a few times you've been able to recover and grow from those situations?

4. Now that you've had a chance to try some positive thinking on your expectations, rewrite your new expectations. (Remember, you don't have to be Pollyanna, just make sure you challenged the validity of your negative thoughts.)

"You gain strength, courage, and confidence by every experience in which you really stop to look fear in the face. You are able to say to yourself, 'I lived through this horror. I can take the next thing that comes along.'"

—ELEANOR ROOSEVELT

CHAPTER TWO

Your Brain on Positivity

In his book, *Hardwiring Happiness*, psychologist Rick Hanson shows us that only one-third of our mood, talents, temperament, and personality are given to us through our genes, whereas we develop the other two-thirds over time. This science invites you to shift the way you think about your life: It's not a race to be won or a problem to be solved, but rather a creative project of becoming, day by day, the person you want to be. Whether you were born with the qualities you emulate or not, you can, through the power of your intention and dedication, create them over time.

This chapter walks you through that creative process. The first step is learning how to work with your thoughts, emotions, and behaviors. We'll begin there, and then you'll put those skills into practice by creating positive stories about your past and optimistic expectations for your future. You'll also learn how to diffuse negative emotions and make the most of positive emotions, and how these emotional experiences influence your perspective and personality over time.

BUT THINKING MAKES IT SO

"... for there is nothing either good or bad,
but thinking makes it so."

—SHAKESPEARE

These wise words from the Bard hold so much truth. The way you think about a situation has everything to do with how you experience it. Researcher Carol Dweck, for example, has demonstrated that people who think of intelligence as a quality that can be increased by hard work make it so: They learn from their mistakes and apply those learnings to future situations.

However, people who think intelligence is a fixed trait also make it so: They write off their mistakes as personal shortcomings and don't grow from their experiences.

Your thoughts, therefore, are extremely powerful, but they're not the only factor influencing your experience. Modern psychology has shown that emotions and actions play an equally critical role. Together, these three factors influence how you feel and what you make of every moment.

But you know who the big boss is? You. With the power of your awareness, you can consciously cultivate certain ways of thinking, emoting, and behaving, giving you the power to change your experiences and your life.

Developing Neuroplasticity

If you eat a whole cake every day for a month, does it change the shape of your body? You bet. Well, just as your daily repetitive choices change your body, they also change your brain. If, for example, every time you get a good grade, your parents treat you to pizza, then that connection would become encoded in your brain. The moment you got an A on your math test (a trigger of achievement), you'd start thinking about the pizza (a thought), craving cheese (an emotion), and texting your mom to place an order for your favorite pie (a behavior). These connections between a specific trigger, thought, emotion, and behavior get stronger in your brain every time you follow this pattern.

If you sign up for the Peace Corps and live in a community where there is no pizza, though, you wouldn't find pizza. Upon receiving positive feedback from your boss (the achievement trigger), you'd still have the thought and emotions driving you to pizza, but without the ability to fulfill that desire, you'd sever the strength of that connection. Instead, you might decide to reward yourself with a local dessert instead (behavior). If you kept repeating this new behavior, your thoughts and emotions would follow suit, and by the end of your service, your brain would have encoded a new connection: achievement trigger = thoughts of desserts, cravings for desserts, and a walk to the local bakery.

This science of neuroplasticity (aka how your brain changes through encoding connections) is the foundation of the path to positivity. As you learn how to intentionally choose the thoughts, emotions, and behaviors that create positivity, and practice them over and over, those connections become encoded in your brain for good and you become a more positive person.

You Are Not What You Think

One of the experiences that brings up negativity for most of us is professional rejection. Imagine that you go into a job interview, give it your all, and then get an email later that day that they selected another candidate. You might immediately think, "I'm not smart enough for that role" or worse, "I should give up." Another person, though, might have a different automatic thought, like "Well, at least I made it to the first round of interviews" or "I wonder what role is a better fit for me."

Either way, the automatic thought is based on the connections you created and repeated with the experience of rejection in the past. If every time you were rejected, or your caretakers blamed you, then that negative connection code would immediately kick in here, too. If you had mentors who taught you to use rejection as an exciting opportunity to learn, however, then that positive connection code would kick in.

What's important to understand is that because your automatic thoughts are a product of your past experiences, they are not necessarily true. Moreover, your brain has a negativity bias, meaning it's more likely to encode negative past experiences than positive ones. Your responsibility, therefore, is not to believe or react to every thought you have, but rather to choose new thoughts that are more accurate and helpful.

Stop Refueling Negative Emotions

The experience of rejection will also trigger automatic emotional reactions. Upon receiving the email, you might immediately feel sad, frustrated, or self-hating. Once again, this immediate experience is a result of your previous programming. Your brain quickly analyzes the situation, scans your relevant memories, and serves up the emotion it frequently connects with rejection.

But it's up to you to decide if you want to further encode that negative emotion with the experience of rejection in your brain. A 2014 *PLOS One* study on the intensity and duration of negative emotions demonstrates that when you ruminate on your emotions, they get stronger and last longer. But when you bring compassionate questioning to your emotional experiences, like asking yourself, "How can I support myself to get through this challenging experience with courage?" they get lighter and fade faster.

Check Your Reaction

When you find out you've been rejected, your brain will also direct you to an automatic reaction based on your past experiences. Perhaps you throw your phone, distract yourself with TV, or refuse to do any more job applications. These behaviors are not helpful in the big picture, though, which is why it's so liberating to consciously choose a different reaction, one that makes you feel proud of the kind of person you are. With that choice, you begin encoding a new, more positive behavior code for dealing with rejection.

DEALING WITH DISTORTED THINKING

Distorted thinking, otherwise known as cognitive distortion, happens when you've made the same types of decisions that result in the same types of negative outcomes over and over again, and your brain learns to develop a pattern of thinking based on these outcomes that is incorrect and unhelpful. For instance, if you decide to go to the gym for the first time in years, and afterward you feel unbelievably sore and horrible, you might say to yourself, "I went to the gym and it was horrible and it's definitely going to feel like this every time I go, so I'll never go again!" This is distorted thinking because your brain has come to the hasty conclusion that this one bad gym experience will be representative of all gym experiences. Challenging these cognitive distortions is key to overcoming your negative beliefs.

Some cognitive distortions include:
- All-or-nothing thinking
- Discounting the positive
- Personalization
- Overgeneralization
- Mental filtering

Let's apply the cognitive distortions to an all-too-familiar scenario, dating:

1. You go on your first date and have a great time, but then you never hear from the other person again. Then you think, "Ugh! That date was a total failure. What a bust."

This is **all-or-nothing thinking**. It's when you look at a situation as black or white, and you can't see the shades of grey.

2. You're telling your date about the business you started. They congratulate you on achieving your most profitable month and you think, "Thanks, but my recent success doesn't really count because I had two terrible months right before that."

This is **discounting the positive**. You take the joy out of your date (and your life) by never letting things be enough and focusing on the negative.

3. Your date gets an urgent phone call and needs to leave early. You think, "What did I do wrong? They're obviously ditching me."

This is **personalization**. You take things personally and make everything your date says and does about you.

4. You go on a date with someone who works in sales, then you find out they have a partner back home. You think, "I'm never dating someone who works in sales again! They're cheaters!"

This is **overgeneralization**. You turn one bad experience into a broad, over-simplified conclusion.

5. When all hope is nearly lost, you finally find a real winner. But, after you've been on multiple dates with this person, you learn they have many of the same hobbies as your ex. You become hyper-focused on this fact alone and completely forget about all of their other unique, positive qualities.

This is **mental filtering**. All of the good things about the person are disregarded because you're focusing on finding the negative aspects of that person.

Which one of these cognitive distortions comes up most frequently for you?

To develop new, healthier, and more balanced ways of perceiving your experience, begin by thinking about a common negative thought you regularly use in your life. Then, after writing that thought down in your journal, write down the answers to the following questions:

1. What negative thought am I having and which of the cognitive distortions is this related to? An easy (and all-too-common) example might be, "I'm lazy," and the cognitive distortion would be **all-or-nothing thinking**.
2. What are three other alternative perspectives to the negative thought? An alternative perspective to the previous example about laziness could include "I don't have the motivation to try harder because I'm not getting enough sleep" or "I haven't yet found an activity or job that is truly meaningful to me."
3. Write down evidence that supports each of these three alternatives. Evidence for the preceding example could include, "I only sleep four to five hours a night because I spend too much time on my phone" or "I haven't yet found an activity or job that is truly meaningful to me because I don't like to take risks and try new things."

Saying "I'm lazy" is easy, but it isn't correct because it disregards so much detail about your situation. Therefore, it's really important to think about the alternative perspectives and their evidence. The evidence helps your brain begin to see a new way of approaching an old problem.

4. Now, choose the most accurate and helpful thought to practice when reflecting on this situation going forward.

COMBATING (BUT NOT AVOIDING) NEGATIVITY

As we covered in chapter 1, paying attention to your negative thoughts, although difficult, can uncover incredibly powerful agents of change. In my work as a coach, I have seen how illuminating negative thoughts has helped my clients recognize distorted thinking and subconscious negative beliefs related to diet, relationships, self-esteem, perfectionism, and poor boundaries, to name a few. And the more my clients observe their negative thoughts, the more they acknowledge their deeper issues, and the more focused and effective their positive thinking practice is toward improving their mind-set, mood, and life. This kind of positive progress gives us tremendous satisfaction and empowers us to live with intention. You, too, will cultivate this capacity. Your goal is not to numb yourself to negativity but to embrace difficult feelings as opportunities for your personal growth and well-being.

Be Realistic

Negative thoughts and feelings play an important role in your life. If your dog passes away, it's okay to feel sad and to spend time grieving his loss. It's also healthy to have feelings that don't make sense to you or that seem "wrong." You might also, for example, feel relieved they're no longer in pain, or more uncomfortably, relieved that you don't have the ongoing responsibility to take care of them, but just remember, be realistic. Thoughts are *just* thoughts, and it's okay to have them, even if they make you uncomfortable.

But what about in other situations, where negativity is not the "appropriate" response? Like when you feel hopeless about your ability to ever find a fulfilling career or hyper-anxious about public speaking? This negativity is helpful, too. It forces you to pay attention to how your thoughts, emotions, and behaviors are impacting your life, and to make beneficial changes. You can't avoid negativity, but you can always use it as an opportunity for self-awareness, growth, and connection.

Stop and Think

When people feel negative emotions, they may do one of two things: ignore them or become overwhelmed by them. But both approaches are unproductive, as ignoring feelings often results in unresolved issues later on and becoming overwhelmed by feelings allows the negativity to take control. Both of these choices allow you to bypass the more challenging, vulnerable option of facing your feelings head-on, but they also rob you of the ability to create change and solve the problem.

DO THIS NOW: TRACKING AND CHANGING NEGATIVE THOUGHT PATTERNS

Oftentimes, the first thoughts and emotions that come to you are not really what's driving your negativity. You need to do the hard work and peel through the layers. This will empower you to make the most meaningful changes to your mind-set.

Look back at the area of your life you chose to create a goal around in chapter 1. What circumstances in that area of your life tend to bring up negativity for you? Focusing on those specific circumstances, get your journal out and write down your answers in the following statements.

5. I feel __(negative emotion)__ because I'm thinking _____
   _____.

6. If this were true, it would mean_____
   _____. Another
   way of stating this is: If this were true, it would bother me
   because_____.

7. Now repeat this statement, over and over. Keep going deeper until you're repeating the same response; that's the core thought underlying your negativity. This is called the "downward arrow" technique because you keep going down, into the layers of your mind, until your reach the heart of the issue.
8. What are three things I can do to change the way I feel in this situation? Specifically, brainstorm what kind of thoughts might help you feel more confident and cared for in this situation, or what behaviors may help you change your perspective.

A DEEPER ISSUE

Although a certain degree of negativity is expected, tolerated, and even helpful, chronic negativity can lead to much more negative outcomes and be a symptom of a more serious mental health issue that cannot be fixed by positive thinking alone. Indeed, studies show that severe depression and anxiety can result from serious illness, hormonal imbalances, nutritional deficiencies, sleep deprivation, traumatic or abusive experiences, and intense personal loss. These issues need to be addressed head-on in order to prevent further negative outcomes.

My own mental health issues, for example, were a result of a complex array of causes. Depression and anxiety ran in my family. My parents struggled with marital conflict and eventually divorced, so my home felt tense and divided. I had a poor self-image and low self-esteem, and I developed an eating disorder when I was 13 years old. Moreover, I later learned that I was dangerously deficient in vitamins B and D, which are two critical nutrients for a healthy-functioning brain.

Positive thinking was an extremely important part of my recovery because it helped me restructure a lot of the negative thoughts that I developed and replace them with positive perspectives on myself and my life. But I also had to address these other issues, with the help of compassionate professionals, in order to support and sustain that positive thinking.

Thinking Through Depression (You Can't)

Depressive disorders are characterized by persistent feelings of sadness, loss of interest in activities you used to enjoy, changes in appetite, loss of energy, troubled or too much sleep, difficulty concentrating, and thoughts of death or suicide. With so much negativity overwhelming your system, forcing yourself to think positively may ultimately have a rebound effect: You try to think positively, but it feels so difficult and unnatural that you just feel even worse about yourself.

So before you work with your thoughts, focus on positive, evidence-based behaviors for improving your depression. A 2016 report in the *Journal of Psychiatric Research* showed, for example, that consistent exercise has a significant positive impact on depression, especially moderate intensity, aerobic exercise. Furthermore, a 2013 study published in *BMC Psychiatry* found that for adults with major depression, eating a Mediterranean diet and eliminating sweets, refined cereals, fried food, fast food, processed meats, and sugary drinks is very helpful in healing. Nutrition is critical because low levels of vitamins B_{12}, B_9 (folate), zinc, and omega-3 are correlated with higher levels of depression, per the *International Journal of Preventive Medicine*.

Finally, try to focus on your strengths. A 2005 article on positive psychology in *American Psychologist* shows that participants in a study who were taught to identify their signature strengths and use them in new ways achieved lasting improvements in depression. If you're not sure what your strengths are, ask a trusted confidant and then apply your strengths to new tasks, paying attention to the positive feedback you get and how good it feels to be using your gifts. For example, if a friend observes that one of your strengths is an overall sense of integrity or morality, try learning about and getting actively involved in a social cause you believe in and see if it sparks joy in your life.

Confronting Anxiety and Worry

Whenever I mention positive thinking to clients who struggle with anxiety, I usually get a response like this: "You want me to work with my thoughts? Ha! They go so fast I can't even catch them much less work with them." Living with anxiety means that you're worrying more often than not and that your thoughts are excessive, intrusive, and difficult to control. Anxiety is also characterized by irritability, difficulty sleeping, impaired concentration, and restlessness. It's extraordinarily difficult to work with these kind of racing thoughts, so research shows it's important to first focus on calming your mind and your body. Proven strategies for soothing and slowing your nervous system include resistance exercise, limiting your caffeine and alcohol intake, and mindfulness practice. Commit to these lifestyle changes first, and once you feel substantial relief, you can begin working with your thoughts.

Getting Help

As you can see, mental health issues are extremely complex and challenging. They are also isolating, making you feel misunderstood, disconnected, and ashamed. That's why the most important step you can take is to connect with someone who can really understand you. Finding a good mentor, therapist, or coach is one of the best things you can do for yourself.

Take time exploring your therapeutic options. Research from *Clinical Psychology Review* in 2010 suggests that cognitive behavioral therapy is a highly effective intervention for anxiety and depression. Outside of therapy, another powerful option is mindfulness-based stress reduction (MBSR), also proven very effective at reducing symptom severity among individuals with a broad range of medical and psychiatric conditions, according to a 2017 review in the *Psychiatric Clinics of North America*.

You can also explore holistic treatments. My practice, for example, combines mindfulness, nutrition, exercise, relationship management, and positive psychology into comprehensive healing programs. Once you climb out of the hole of anxiety or depression (and I know you will!), the positive thinking skills you'll learn in this book will feel much more accessible.

NO REGRETS

I resented my parents for many years. I believed because of their marital issues, I developed the classic issues associated with an unstable childhood: anxiety, distrust of other people, a nagging sense of rootlessness, and tremendous insecurity. These issues negatively affected my relationships, my self-worth, and my mental health. I found good company in this mentality, too. Blaming our parents for our issues is at the heart of a great deal of therapy. And it was a nice break, for once, from blaming myself for everything. Ultimately, though, I realized that lingering on the past and trying to find fault and place blame, either on myself or my parents, made it very hard to maintain a positive mind-set.

Reflecting on our past is important because it gives us important insights into our current patterns of thinking, feeling, and behaving. But there are much more effective ways to reflect than simply dwelling on resentment and blame. Let's take a look at a couple of helpful ways you can process your past in order to overcome negativity.

Let the Past Pass

When I practiced the downward arrow technique (the practice you just learned), I figured out that at the heart of all my parental resentment was the belief that if I'd had a different upbringing as a child, I'd have a better life. This type of thinking is indeed why most of us feel so haunted by our past: We have an image of some ideal person we're supposed to be and an ideal life we're supposed to have, and when we do or experience something that throws us off from that ideal, we refuse to let go of that story because it makes us feel like we can prevent it from happening and hurting us again. The truth, though, is that if we *overfocus* on the negatives in our past, the more those connections become hardwired in our brain and set us up to repeat, rather than avoid, the same issues in the future.

But didn't I just talk about how acknowledging the negative is important, too? Yes, absolutely. But staying in that space of negativity, wallowing in it, brooding and ruminating in it, is incredibly unhealthy. So instead of settling into regret about your mistakes or resentment toward others' mistakes, take positive actions to create a better future. For example, if you're approaching the end of your career and you realize you chose the wrong line of work, make the most of your retirement by pursuing the degree of your dreams. If you're a parent who was so preoccupied with work and the pursuit of success that you missed countless once-in-a-lifetime moments with your child, make the changes now to reorganize your work-life balance. These concrete experiences of positive progress not only feel rewarding but also help put an end to the pain from your past.

Talking to Your Thoughts

How are negative thoughts about your past inhibiting your ability to fulfill the goal you set out to achieve in chapter 1? Whether you're blaming yourself or another person, acknowledge those thoughts and try having a conversation with them in which you look for the reason why these mistakes were committed in the first place and how you can prevent them in the future. If, for example, your thoughts are saying, "You didn't watch your diet for all those years and now you have heart disease," you can then ask, "What fear or need was driving my behavior to not watch my diet? What didn't I understand then? What support did I lack?"

Having a dialogue with your thoughts is a great way to reflect without regret because, first, it allows you to separate yourself from your thoughts and see them more objectively and, second, learn from the actual content of the dialogue.

Shoulda, Woulda, Coulda

When I dialogued with my negative thoughts about my parents, I realized that they, just like me, were humans wrought with fragilities, anxieties, and unmet needs. They, too, were loved imperfectly by their parents. And they were doing the very best they could, with what they had. Within that context, I've slowly taken my resentment of what I didn't get from them and replaced it with appreciation for what I did get (including the very gift of life, of being born).

The more you run this thought exercise about your past, the more you learn to let go of the shoulda-woulda-couldas and accept the fact of the human condition: We can't always make the right choices. Sometimes we lack the information we need, or we don't have enough time to consider the options, or we get overwhelmed by our emotions and baggage. Own this reality, learn from your mistakes, and move forward. Know that the only thing you can change about your past is the way it affects you in the present.

Because sitting with negativity is usually a heavy, uncomfortable experience, it's tempting to try to ignore it and hope it will just go away. But when we avoid negative thoughts and emotions, they tend to lurk in the background, waiting for the right moment to return. Let's explore how avoidance of negativity deprives you of opportunities to grow.

What is a common negative thought—one you wish you could just get rid of and often try to suppress—that you have in relationship to the goal you're working on in this book? In your journal, reflect on the following questions to see how this avoidance is affecting you.

1.   What are your favorite strategies for escaping? How do you distract or numb yourself? What places, people, and activities do you avoid in order to keep the thought away? How might you use food, alcohol, drugs, or digital devices to suppress the thought?

2.   How effective are your avoidance strategies in the short term? How about the long term? Do they help you create a more fulfilling life?

3.   What are the costs of avoiding the negative thought in terms of your time, energy, money, health, relationships, and vitality?

4.   How would your life improve if you dialogued with this negative thought with kindness and committed to learning from it?

A NEW NARRATIVE

As you begin to confront the negative thoughts about the past, you make space in your mind for new, more empowering stories. For example, "I drove her away by being too needy" can with time become "I'm learning how to get support from my romantic partner." "I got the wrong degree and wasted my life" can become "It took me 15 years to discover my life's calling, but I never gave up, and now I'm on my way."

Adopting and practicing these new positive thoughts affects your emotions and your behaviors. You'll feel better about everything that has happened up to now, and you'll stop shunning the people and situations that evoked mistakes and failure. This is why positive thinking is such a transformative tool: It gives you control over your experience rather than letting your experiences control you, and this power of creating new narratives emerges when you look to the future.

To begin to create a new narrative, look to optimism, your own strengths, and a sense of intention.

Optimism Is Not Ridiculous

Anna, a writer and former client of mine, submitted her manuscript to two publishers and was declined both times. As she prepared to approach another publisher, she kept telling herself that she would probably be rejected again, and that she'd be forced to stay in her dead-end job forever. In response to her negative thinking, I asked her how the negative thoughts affected her emotions and behavior. "They make me feel sad and heavy, which makes me want to give up on this whole thing," she said.

I reminded Anna that she couldn't control the publishers' responses, but she could at least control her thoughts, her emotions, and her behaviors. My client wasn't convinced, however. "What am I supposed to do? Just trick myself into believing that this time my manuscript will be accepted, even though the experiences from my past predict failure?"

Actually, research suggests that being optimistic is not only logical but also practical. In an article in the *Psychologist-Manager*

Journal in 2007, researchers examined studies on entrepreneurs from over a 25-year period and concluded that dispositional optimism—the global expectation that good things will be plentiful in the future and bad things scarce—is largely correlated to success. So, cultivating a positive perspective about the future will actually help you create a more successful future. This is because of the way that your thinking affects your emotions and behaviors. Expecting good things keeps you motivated and hard-working; expecting bad things zaps your energy and makes you want to give up.

Look to Yourself

Anna persisted: "But what if the publisher rejects me? I don't want to have to feel that disappointment again." This is the reason most people cling to pessimism: It's protective. If we keep our expectations low enough, we'll never have to bear the discomfort of disappointment or failure. This rationale, however, comes from a flawed deterministic viewpoint that posits we can't control or change the way we feel. By now you know this isn't accurate, and you don't have to wallow in disappointment. Instead, you can work with your thoughts, your emotions, and your behaviors to change your experience.

"What are some things in your control that can help you overcome that disappointment?" I asked her. "Well, I can remember that even J.K. Rowling, my favorite author, was rejected twelve times by publishers before finding success. I can go to yoga, which always helps me release my stress. And I can reach out to a friend in publishing for help," she said. Anna's response is a great example of how one can maintain their power, even in discouraging situations. If you feel emotionally overwhelmed, look to yourself and the aspects of your experience that you *can* control.

Find the Fun

Another reason we tend to make negative predictions about the future is our brains' built-in negativity bias, which makes us more likely to pay attention to negative experiences than positive ones. If you did 10 things well today and made one mistake, you're still more likely to be ruminating on the mistake as you lie in bed at night. And the more you focus on the negativity from your past, the more your brain predicts those experiences in the future.

Thank goodness for neuroplasticity. You can gradually change your negativity bias and become more optimistic by intentionally focusing on small, positive experiences throughout your day. I call this the "face it, feed it, feel it" technique. First, face it: Pay attention to your positive experience. This can be something as simple as a relaxing breath or a stranger's smile on the subway. Then, feed it: Enrich the experience by thinking more fun, uplifting thoughts about it. You might say to yourself, "It's amazing how just one deep breath can make me feel so good." And finally, feel it: Get into the positive emotions, feel them in your body, and really let them sink in. Imagine them like a bubble bath, covering your entire body with sensations of warmth and ease.

A CAN-DO ATTITUDE

Why do we exercise? For at least two reasons: First, it can feel amazing to get your body moving and your blood pumping. Second, for the long-term benefits—the more you work out, the stronger and toned and your whole body becomes. Similarly, every time you practice positive thinking, it's like you're taking your mind to the gym. Not only does it feel great to create a positive personal narrative and embrace optimism, but it also makes you a stronger, healthier person, and more resilient and resourceful in challenging times. When practiced over and over, positivity morphs from a temporary state into a lasting personality trait.

The Mental and the Physical

Many people dismiss positivity as a frivolous quality—it's great if it happens, but it's not important for real-world success. Serious adults focus on cultivating grit, work ethic, self-reliance, and willpower; positivity is child's play, they say. And, on some level, it's true: Positive emotions *do* make us lighter and more playful. But these uplifting experiences are far from frivolous; indeed, they are the portal to wisdom and well-being.

When you're consumed in negativity, you lose perspective. Stress hormones cut off communication from your brain's prefrontal cortex, which is responsible for self-control, compassion, empathy, and rational decision making. This disconnection leaves you with a more primitive form of communication and action that derives from your limbic brain, which is only adept at extreme reactions like fight, flight, and freeze. If your spouse says something hurtful, for example, and you become consumed in anger, you're unable to think about the big picture, like all the positive experiences you've had together, or all the sacrifices you've made for one another, or of how they might be feeling; rather, the only thing you can think about is your spouse's hurtful comment, so you're prone to overreact in ways you'll later regret. The same thing happens when you feel stressed or ashamed: You lose access to perspective and respond in unskillful ways.

Positive emotions, however, like joy, hope, awe, and safety, help reestablish communication between the prefrontal and limbic parts of your brain. In other words, you regain access to your emotional intelligence and critical thinking skills, and these wiser, more evolved parts of your brain can soothe and support the part that handles stress. If you can pause your argument with your spouse and tap into these positive emotions, you become empowered to look at the big picture and respond in ways that align with your values and help you achieve your long-term goals.

Be Like a Child at Play

Positive emotions also enable meaningful connection. Research by psychologist Barbara Fredrickson shows that within safe, close relationships, "joy sparks the urge to play, interest sparks the urge to explore, contentment sparks the urge to savor, and love sparks a recurring cycle of each of these urges." These positive interpersonal experiences are critical for the success of your relationships. For example, in order to have a long and happy marriage, research shows that couples must exchange positive interest, affection, and appreciation toward one another five times more than negative emotions. Even business teams that exchange primarily positive emotions, such as encouragement and appreciation, are more successful than teams that share mostly disapproval or cynicism.

Improve Resiliency

Positivity, therefore, helps you build emotional regulation skills and stronger relationships. These are two of the most important factors contributing to resilience, which is why, in the face of adversity, positive people tend to bounce back better and grow from the experience. We all go through tough times: layoffs happen, markets crash, relationships end, and people die. Positivity is not about glossing over the challenges these experiences bring up. Rather, it's about intentionally cultivating positive emotions in order to access your prefrontal cortex so that you can effectively and empathically problem solve. Moreover, if you regularly practice feeling and sharing positive emotions, you're more likely to tap into relationships for advice and support to help you overcome adversity. This is why the work you're doing in this book is not just a way of improving your momentary state of mind; it's preventive medicine that keeps you healthy and resourceful in even the most challenging times.

POSITIVITY IN PRACTICE

Your life is one big creative project. In every moment, you create your experience by working with your thoughts, emotions, and behaviors. The more you rehearse these connections, the more they become your habitual way of thinking, feeling, and responding. Over time, these habits then create your narrative, mind-set, and personality, and they influence your long-term relationships and coping styles.

When cultivating thoughts, emotions, and behaviors, therefore, it's important to keep your goals in mind. Negative thoughts aren't inherently bad, but they are often based on cognitive distortions, and they aren't usually helpful at face value. Before changing them, then, make sure to use the downward arrow technique to identify the core thought, and then dialogue with it, so that you can learn about what needs may be unmet or what support you require to continue moving toward your goal. Then you can choose new, more helpful and accurate thought patterns to practice going forward.

Because of the negativity bias, it's also important to conscientiously notice good things and cultivate, enrich, and share positive experiences. Let's do that together now.

Reflecting on your goal in this book, what is one example of progress you've already made? When you're thinking about your positive progress, how does that make you feel? Joyful, hopeful, or maybe confident? Allow yourself to feed and feel this positive experience for 30 seconds. Now, thinking about this positivity, how are you inclined to act? Perhaps you want to be playful and celebrate your success with a victory dance, or perhaps you want to be generous and share your joy with others. Embrace these instincts, for they will help you create a better mind and life.

"I wish for a world where everyone understands that discomfort is the price of legendary. And fear is just growth coming to get you."

—ROBIN SHARMA

CHAPTER THREE

Living Your Values

Happiness doesn't equal satisfaction, but that's not what we've been led to believe. Everywhere we go, we are inundated by messages telling us that a product or a program or a personal achievement will bring us a feeling of happiness so pure, so fulfilling that we won't want anything else (for at least a moment). We keep striving and pushing for more, hungry for happiness. And when unhappiness inevitably rears its ugly head, we buckle at the knees, develop cognitive distortions to help us cope, and blame ourselves for not feeling better.

I have seen this destructive cycle unfold in my life and the lives of my coaching clients. But I have learned that each day I live my values and remain committed to positive growth and change, I feel deeply *satisfied*, even if I'm not happy at that point in time. Positive emotions, like happiness, have many significant benefits and can lead to numerous wonderful outcomes, and positive thinking can lead you to a life of meaning, one in which you can handle the inevitable ups and downs of being human.

In this chapter, you'll learn to go beyond your search for happiness by defining and employing your values to create lasting fulfillment in your life that can sustain you in the long run. You'll also learn to move through some of the discomfort that may arise from this process in order to gain a better sense of self-direction and agency in your life.

HAPPINESS ISN'T REQUIRED

Imagine if the only emotion you could ever feel was happiness. This might sound like the ultimate blessing, but what if your partner cheats on you or your best friend tells you they've been diagnosed with cancer? In these situations, happiness isn't the appropriate emotional response. In fact, if you did feel happy, you might ignore your marriage issues or dismiss your friend's need for compassion.

Moreover, research shows that if your only goal is to feel happy all the time, then it actually has the reverse effect. A 2011 study published in *Emotion* found that people who valued happiness more tended to experience less of it, be less satisfied with their lives, report lower psychological well-being, and greater levels of depression symptoms. This paradoxical effect occurs because if you value happiness itself, then your expectations for happiness are high, and whenever an experience brings up other emotions, you become disappointed, thinking something is wrong. You're also more prone to glossing over negative emotions, rather than learning from them. Over time, these factors actually decrease your overall happiness.

It's not uncommon for me to talk with my coaching clients about the differences between happiness and satisfaction. For example, a client once said, "Caitlin, I know that helping people is part of being a coach. But I also know that it's important to be as happy as possible. Isn't it hard to be happy when you're talking about people's fears and problems all day? How do you do both at the same time?" And although the client asked an important question about how to balance satisfaction, career, and happiness, she forgot an essential point: You don't always need to be happy and being as happy as possible can be far less important than being satisfied. And with satisfaction, happiness can follow.

Happiness itself, therefore, is not a helpful goal. But often, it is the by-product of something much more substantial—meaning. When people reflect on the greatest moments of their lives, they most often recount memories in which they overcame an obstacle, achieved a difficult milestone, or contributed to the life of another in need. These accomplishments include many happy moments but also involve vulnerability, discomfort, and challenges. For example, in a 2014 study published in the journal *Demography*, researchers demonstrated that peoples' happiness actually decreases just after they have their first child.

Similarly, when you're learning to play a new instrument, the early days are filled with mistakes and confusion. However, every parent and musician would agree that the moments of unhappiness pale in comparison to the meaning and fulfillment that come, in part, from being resilient in those tough times and marching forward toward the goal of playing that new instrument.

Life Is Real

Meaning, then, can lead to satisfaction. And satisfaction can lead to happiness.

The making of anything meaningful will, inevitably, involve ups and downs. Most of us understand this principle intellectually, and yet the moment difficulty knocks on our door, we label it as bad or wrong, try to escape or change the situation, and get caught up in questions about our happiness. If you're feeling lonely, for example, your automatic response might be to blame yourself and think that something is wrong with you because you're unhappy. If you're feeling motivated to change, you might hurry to invest in a self-improvement program which you believe will somehow make you more likeable. And if you're feeling especially unmotivated, you might let those negative thoughts convince you that you're not worthy of having friends and then not take any action to meet people.

Much of the pain we feel in life is because we work so hard to avoid it; we're not realistic about life's ups and downs. Everyone on this planet has periods of loneliness, sadness, confusion, and lack of motivation. We blame ourselves for having these feelings, which only leads to more negativity. Moreover, when you're busy pushing away your negative emotions, you aren't giving yourself the space to learn about your values and needs. And when you can't learn from your negative feelings, they tend to keep coming back with greater intensity, until you can receive their important messages.

Accepting Your Emotions

Perhaps you're feeling a little confused right now. I spent the last chapter telling you that your negative thoughts are often untrue and unhelpful, and in this chapter, I'm telling you that negativity is a part of life and that accepting these experiences is a crucial part of cultivating meaning and positivity. But there is, in fact, no contradiction here, because there's a big difference between *acknowledging* your negative thoughts and *believing* your negative thoughts. For example, I can acknowledge that I am having strong negative thoughts about my capacity to succeed in a new role at work, but that doesn't mean that I have to believe those thoughts. As strange as it might sound, thoughts themselves can be inaccurate, so we can't always believe the negative ones, even if we really want to.

Therefore, an acceptance of having negative thoughts is not resignation; it's just an open-hearted presence to your inner experience. It's the choice to nestle your negative emotions in a larger attitude of self-care. As someone who hasn't spent more than three years in the same city since my teens, I sometimes feel lonely. Over the years, the best way I have found to navigate this feeling is by acknowledging it honestly and telling myself it's okay to feel that way. This broadens my emotional experience so that I feel both lonely and cared for simultaneously. Holding a challenging emotion with kindness is kind of like a bittersweet good-bye: You feel sad things are ending but also grateful for the experience you had, and overall, you're able to maintain a positive, solution-focused mind-set.

Understanding, Not Avoiding

As previously discussed, accepting your negative emotions also keeps the communication between your limbic brain and pre-frontal cortex flowing, so that you can broaden your perspective on your experience and understand how to address the underlying issue, rather than just cover over your feelings. On the other hand, resistance, which usually takes the form of blame, regret, and grasping for control, cuts you off from this wisdom.

Psychologist Tara Brach is a master of self-acceptance. This exercise is an adaptation of her teachings, tailored around the acronym PAIN, so that you remember to use it whenever you're experiencing difficult emotions.

Pause. Set aside a few moments to practice self-care. Bathroom breaks are encouraged in social situations.

Accept. Say something like, "I open my heart to this experience and all the difficult emotions it entails."

Investigate. Get to the heart of the matter. What memories or thoughts are fueling these negative emotions? What are you believing about the future? Is this all true, or might there be other, more helpful ways you can think about this situation?

Nurse. Figure out what you can do, think, or remember to gently nurse your heart back to health and allow you to move forward gracefully.

When you embrace your pain in this way, you learn from your negative emotions and grow your ability to cope in healthy ways.

VALUES MATTER

When you embrace your negative emotions, one of the biggest benefits is that you gain insight into who and what really matters to you, to understand your values. My client Mike, for example, lost his brother when he was 18 years old.

In addition to his grief, Mike was plagued by feelings of remorse that he had not spent more quality time with his sibling. By practicing PAIN, he realized how important family and authenticity were to him, and he rearranged his life accordingly, spending a lot more time with those he loved and having more honest conversations with them.

Knowing what really matters to you is the key to creating a meaningful life. On the path to positivity, you make the choice to use every experience—the good, the bad, or the ugly—to gain insight into what really matters to you and what aligns with your personal values.

What We Mean by "Values"

What's more important, enforcing justice or creating a culture of mercy? Being flexible or following the rules? That depends on your values, on the fundamental ideals that are most important to you. Many of these values were instilled in you by your family and culture. For example, my husband, who was raised in India, learned to value community. When he moved to America and saw people jogging by themselves, he said, "I feel so bad! Why are these people all alone?" I explained that many Americans often value individualism and independence.

The values you were taught growing up, however, are not necessarily ones that you agree with today. As a kid, I learned to value intelligence and hard work, which meant I hustled to become a star student and get into an Ivy League school. When I got older, however, I realized that these achievements didn't fulfill me because my values were different from those of my upbringing. I care far more about compassion, creativity, and nature than I do about intelligence and hard work. When I stopped pushing myself so hard to get perfect results and focused instead on being compassionate and creative in the process, I became a much more positive, fulfilled person.

What values are important in your family and culture? How have these values impacted your choices? Do they resonate with you today?

Making Meaning

Think of your values as your map to making a meaningful life. For example, if you value collaboration but you work in a competitive sales role in which you're pitted against your coworkers, you're going to feel frustrated and unfulfilled. You'd be much more fulfilled in your company's marketing team who work together to achieve the end revenue goal.

Similarly, when you befriend people who share your values, you're more likely to feel a sense of belonging, which is the cornerstone of meaningful relationships. Intimate relationships also thrive when both partners have a sense of shared meaning, according to research conducted by the Gottman Institute. For example, my clients Emily and Chrissy were opposite in almost every way, but they both valued learning and compromise, so they found meaning in showing up for each other's passions and hobbies. And the same goes for business: A 2011 study in the *Journal of Applied Behavioral Studies* demonstrated that business teams that exchange primarily positive emotions, such as encouragement and appreciation, are more successful than teams that share mostly disapproval or cynicism.

It's the Little Things

Beyond big decisions like your relationships and career, your values also help infuse positivity into your everyday life. Let's say it's time to do your taxes and you want to escape the drudgery of form filling. If you value companionship, you can make a "tax date" with a friend and commiserate together while trudging through the forms. If you value spending time outside, you might take your laptop out to your backyard or a public park to make the task less onerous.

In fact, you can positively change your life right now by simply going through your regular task list in a way that aligns with your values. Maybe you value self-reflection and choose to take the long way home from work for a few extra minutes of alone time. Or you value playfulness and purchase silly gag gifts for friends' birthdays. What would tomorrow be like if you committed to bringing your values into everything you do? How can you make your experiences more meaningful by aligning your thoughts, feelings, and behaviors with your values?

Values =/= Goals

Because living in alignment with your values is an ongoing source of meaning and positivity, your goals should be in service to your values. If they're not, then actualizing those goals won't bring you the satisfaction you're searching for. Moreover, your values can help you prioritize your goals. If you're not sure which goals will help you most on your path to positivity, look at which of your values is most underserved right now and prioritize the goal that will help you fix that gap.

What goals did you write down in the first chapter of this book? Are they in alignment with your values? How can you change what you're trying to achieve or how you're trying to achieve it, so that it is in service to your values?

Get out your journal and answer the following questions to learn more about what matters most to you. Remember, you're the only person who's going to see these answers. Don't write the answers that you think you should put down or the ones your mom or your boss would be proud to read. Tell your personal truth.

1. Identify the three most fulfilling experiences in your life. Describe what you were you doing, where, and with whom. What made it such a fulfilling experience?

2. Identify the three most frustrating times of your life. What felt wrong about those situations or experiences? Was something missing? Why were they so frustrating?

3. Who do you want to come to your funeral? What do you want each of those people to say about you at your funeral?

4. What would you do if you knew you could not fail?

5. What are the kinds of activities or experiences in which you lose yourself completely—where the mental chatter stops, and you're fully present, enjoying the moment? What about these experiences locks you into the moment?

6. What's the most meaningful thing in your life right now? Why?

Now read over your answers. What patterns do you notice about what you care about, what motivates and fills you? Perhaps your greatest successes involved helping another person, or you felt most fulfilled after launching a new initiative at your company. All of these answers offer clues as to what your values might be.

For each response, note two associated values in the margin. Then tally up which values came up most consistently for you. Which three values rise to the top? These are your core values.

PUSHING PAST DISCOMFORT

If you're ever in New York in January, go out to the beach in Brooklyn and you'll find the Coney Island Polar Bears, a group of very brave humans, going for a swim in the bone-chilling Atlantic Ocean.

Why would you subject yourself to such an excruciating experience? Because this is the science of success: The more you practice tolerating discomfort, the more confident you'll feel in confronting new challenges. Think, for example, about the inspiring goals you're working toward. Deep down, you know these goals will enrich your life with meaning, especially now that you've made sure they align with your core values. But the bigger you dare to dream, the greater the discomfort you'll endure.

For example, if you're in the midst of a relationship conflict, you can keep quiet in the name of "keeping the peace" or you can put your heart on the line, stand up for your needs, and admit your mistakes. The second option is uncomfortable as hell. When you share your vulnerability, your partner might respond condescendingly, criticize your anxiety, or tell you that your needs are ridiculous. But if you're committed to creating a meaningful relationship, you must embrace this discomfort and continue working toward the deep understanding you crave.

The same is true in your career, your friendships, and your lifestyle. Asking for help, taking a risk, learning a new skill, changing your mind, standing your ground—all of these tasks involve the possibility of failure, judgment, and rejection. If you truly want to live a fulfilling life, you must prioritize progress over comfort.

It's Often Fleeting

Swimming through the sea of discomfort is not easy, but the good news is that the sea isn't always freezing; the discomfort comes in waves. Remember, your brain is biased against ambiguity: Anything that involves unfamiliarity or uncertainty, even things that are good for you, will trigger your brain to shoot out a stress response and put you on high alert; you'll feel anticipation or angst and your heart rate will pick up. This is where most people get tripped up. We think that if we feel the sensations of the stress response, it means something bad is happening and we should turn back. In fact, discomfort is a sign that you're in unfamiliar territory and it's time to pay attention so you can skillfully navigate your way through.

When a wave of discomfort hits, when you're feeling embarrassed, nervous, or overwhelmed, start by slowing your breathing. Take just six breaths per minute, with five-second inhales and five-second exhales. According to research published in the journal *Applied Psychophysiology and Biofeedback*, this kind of breathing increases relaxation, reduces stress, and promotes mindfulness and positive energy. Once your stress response comes down, you've created the conditions in which you can start listening to your prefrontal cortex and interrupt the emotional current.

Be Flexible

After relaxing your body, how do you interrupt an emotional current? You guessed it: positive thinking. Ask yourself: What am I believing about this situation? Are all of these thoughts really true? Do these thoughts make me feel cared for and confident? If not, what is a more helpful perspective on this situation that will empower me to keep making progress toward my goals?

This kind of psychological flexibility—that is, the willingness to ask questions and try on a different perspective that is more helpful to you—is the ultimate skill on the path to positivity because it keeps you moving forward. Everybody enjoys positive thinking, but when discomfort strikes, they toss these skills away like an empty water bottle and, therefore, they never reach their destination. That's why we ride the waves.

Remember Your Resilience

Remember, positive thinking is not about faking good feelings. If you're freezing your butt off, don't think, "I'm the warmest person in the world right now." That's not a helpful thought; it's a downright lie. A better alternative is remembering your resilience. Chances are you've overcome something like this or worse in the past. You've endured heartbreak, been rejected by employers, and made a total fool of yourself in public. What strengths and resources from that experience can you tap into here? If you read through your list of achievements, I bet you'll notice a theme: breakdown leads to breakthrough. What other evidence demonstrates that you're strong enough to work through this discomfort?

THE LAW OF ATTRACTION—IS IT A THING?

Are you scared of embracing your negative thoughts and emotions because you believe that by thinking about negative things, you'll manifest more of those negative things in your life? You're not alone. This fear comes from the "law of attraction," which, in short, asserts that your thoughts create your reality.

There's a lot of debate about the science of the law of attraction, but we do know that your thoughts affect your emotions and your behaviors. Research published in 2018 in the journal *Self and Identity*, for example, demonstrates that positive, self-affirming thoughts help bolster your feelings of self-worth and make you respond more constructively to threats. Negative, self-doubting thoughts on the other hand, have the opposite effect: They make you feel bad. In this very real sense, then, your thoughts do influence your reality.

There is also ample evidence that people who visualize their future are more successful at bringing that future into existence. Research published in 2016 in the journal *Basic and Applied Social Psychology* summarized multiple studies documenting how visualization "programs" the body and mind to improve performance in athletic, academic, and work contexts. Science can't confirm that these are actually thoughts condensing into solid form, but when you focus on something over and over, you hardwire that pattern in your brain and create automatic thoughts, emotions, and behaviors. These automatic patterns shape your perspective and experience in every moment and, consequently, contribute to the reality you create. Remember: This doesn't mean you should be afraid to feel negative feelings. If you try to bypass your negativity, you don't resolve it and it continues to influence your experience. However, if you dialogue with your negative thoughts, or practice acceptance with your negative emotions, you not only help resolve the negativity for good, but you also begin to develop new, positive ways of thinking and feeling, which will lead to good things.

YOU GET TO CHOOSE

Let's review three core positivity concepts we've discussed thus far. First, every experience consists of thoughts, feelings, and behaviors. For example, a negative thought like "I'm terrible at public speaking because I get nervous standing in front of all those people" can lead to a negative feeling such as "I feel incompetent because I can't talk without freezing or messing up." This negative feeling can lead to a negative behavior like "I am not going to apply for a job that sounds perfect for me because I might have to do a lot of presentations for people." Each time this pattern is repeated, it becomes harder to break. But you can create positive experiences by interrupting your habituated patterns and choosing alternatives that help you reach your goals. For instance, you can change your thinking to "In the past, I haven't felt comfortable speaking in front of large groups, but it's normal to feel that way, and I can sign up for a public speaking class to gain confidence," which will have a dramatic impact on the way you feel and behave. You might think, "I feel more confident and prepared now that I have a plan of action to improve" and so you go out and apply for that awesome job that includes a lot of presentations.

Second, positive emotions have tremendous mental, physical, and social benefits. The more you enrich these experiences, the more you'll reap the benefits. As you continually practice positivity, you'll overcome the negativity bias and create a more positive default through neuroplasticity.

Third, you're not seeking empty or transient emotional highs; you're pursuing enduring fulfillment. This means your goals must align with your values, and you need to be willing to deal with discomfort and face your negativity head-on. Every experience is an opportunity to create meaning and growth, and positivity requires you to embrace reality as it ensues.

These three concepts make you a remarkably powerful person because they give you the tools to change your brain and, consequently, your life. But with great power comes great responsibility. Now that you have the knowledge and tools, you must take ownership of your relationship with your experiences.

How You Want to Be Seen

Recently, one of my clients, Katelyn, complained, "I want my husband to do his housework, but I'm afraid that if I keep reminding him, he'll think I'm a nag."

This is the most popular way that people give up their power. They fear that other people will judge them, so they forgo their own needs. Self-sacrifice, though, is based on an inaccurate understanding of human relationships: that the only way to get people to like you is by putting their needs before yours.

To be a genuinely positive person, replace your self-sacrifice with a commitment to your core values. Katelyn values kindness and trust, so she laid these values on the table with her husband, saying, "I know that you don't like cleaning, and to be kind to you, I do a lot of your chores. But I'm not being kind to myself because this always leaves me exhausted. Plus, I end up secretly resenting you, which erodes the trust between us. Let's brainstorm ways we can manage housework that is kind to both of us and creates more transparency."

You cannot control other people's opinions of you, but you can communicate the values you're committed to carrying out in your relationships.

What Your Life Looks Like

> *"But what if the other person doesn't change, despite you communicating your values?"*

Trying to change other people who don't want to change is a fast track to resentment, despair, and anxiety. Instead, focus on what's in your control and take responsibility for sticking to your values no matter what. When my client Matt told his boss that he needed a phone break on Saturdays to spend time with family, his boss scoffed: "You either value success or you take phone-free Saturdays. Not both." Matt explained that he valued success and family and communicated several ideas for how he could honor both of these values. Unfortunately, his boss wouldn't budge.

If Matt had surrendered and worked every Saturday for the rest of his life, he'd feel like a helpless victim. But he's on the path to positivity, so instead, he took responsibility for his experience by committing to his values. He got a new job and made it clear to his employer that weekends are for family. It's important to note that in the case of this scenario, Matt had to deal with a lot of negative thoughts during this period of time when he was making the decision to find work elsewhere. Lining up your values against your negative thoughts can be very uncomfortable, and Matt had to sit with the discomfort, but the end result truly aligned with his values, which made him feel stronger and more fulfilled.

How You Spend Your Time

*"But if I commit to my values and stop
sacrificing myself for others, people won't like
me and I'll end up all alone."*

If this thought has crossed your mind, take a deep breath and have some self-compassion. It's horrible to live with the fear that being true to yourself will result in abandonment, but the truth is that some people will fall out of your life when you take responsibility for living true to your values. However, do you know what else will happen? New people will show up, and these people will accept and even share your values.

Yes, you'll have to deal with the discomfort of disappointing other people. But in return, you'll meet your soulmates—people who appreciate you and respect your priorities—and spend time doing things you actually enjoy. I'd say that's a pretty good tradeoff, wouldn't you?

Your life, your time, and your thoughts are in your hands. How will you choose to spend them, my courageous reader?

DO THIS NOW: TAKE RESPONSIBILITY

The most important decision you'll ever make is when you decide to take responsibility for your relationship to all of your experience. I call this "radical responsibility."

In your journal, begin by reflecting on all the reasons you feel it's difficult or impossible for you to achieve the goal you set earlier in this book. Don't judge yourself while you're doing this or hold back anything that comes to mind. Remember, negative thoughts aren't bad; they help create self-awareness and direct your personal development efforts going forward.

Common responses include: She'll think I don't love her. He'll fire me. She won't want to be my friend. He'll lose respect for me. I'm cursed. I'm not smart enough. I don't have the right connections. I don't have time. I'll make less money.

Then use positive thinking to approach this goal with an attitude of radical responsibility.

1. Are the disempowering stories you just wrote down really 100 percent true? What evidence do you have to back them up? Are there any exceptions or instances of this not being true?

2. Are there any more realistic, helpful perspectives you could nurture about your situation? (*Hint*: Remember resilience, optimism, and positive self-talk.)

3. What's in your control?

Can you have a discussion with another person about your values and needs?

Can you leave or change your relationship with the person or organization that's currently an obstacle for you?

Can you let go of someone else's opinion of you and focus on the positive experience of living true to your values?

Can you change the way you're approaching or measuring this goal in order to bring down your resistance and keep moving forward?

Finally, summarize your new action plan, powered by radical responsibility. What new thoughts, feelings, and behaviors will you commit to in order to achieve what matters most?

APPRECIATE YOU

With all this talk about taking radical responsibility for your life, your thoughts, and your choices, you might be feeling a little freaked out. Taking responsibility can easily morph into blaming yourself whenever anything goes wrong.

However, responsibility is about feeling empowered to make progress toward your goals by focusing on what you can control. If you're weighing yourself down with blame, you're not empowered, and when you feel bad about yourself, your energy dwindles. Research by Brené Brown shows that blame and accountability have an inverse relationship; you can either spend your energy raging at your wrongs, or you can dedicate your energy toward the vulnerable process of trying (and maybe failing) again.

On the path to positivity, *responsibility = acceptance + non-judgment + taking action.*

When something goes wrong, practice acceptance by being willing to see reality as it is. Then, as if you were a scientist in a lab, analyze the result. How did different variables like your thoughts, feelings, behaviors, and environment influence your outcome? What variables will you play with to get a better outcome next time? Remember, your life is a creative project, not a race to be won.

Avoid the Comparison Trap

If, during your experimentation process, you see that your neighbor has already achieved the outcome you're working toward, you might feel jealous or discouraged. However, radical responsibility directs your energy back to what you can control, and that always starts with your thoughts.

When you find yourself falling into this comparison trap, there are two positive thinking strategies that will keep you moving forward. First, remember your values; those are your primary metrics of success. If your goal is to become the human resources director at a Fortune 500 company and you value wellness, travel, and kindness, you may fulfill your goal a little slower than your B-school classmate who values efficiency and recognition. That doesn't mean you're failing. Instead, it means you're pursuing your goals in your unique way and in accordance with your values.

Second, transform your comparison into motivation. We feel more motivated when we believe our goals are attainable. If your best friend gets married, see it as a reminder that finding your soul mate is possible, no matter how many bad dates you've been on. Be inspired by the successes of other people, letting them motivate you to keep going. Because of your unique values, you'll reach your goals in a different way and on a different timeline, but you *will* get there.

You're Only Human

> *"But what if I don't live true to my own values? I've sabotaged my own success over and over, and I'm responsible for my failure. How can I not hate myself?"*

The truth is, nobody creates pain unless they are in pain. Pause and let that sink in for a moment. Now explore more deeply what is driving all of your "self-sabotage" and mistakes. If you're hurting someone you love, did you act out of hurt and insecurity? If you're addicted to food, drugs, or alcohol, what need are you trying to satisfy? What fear are you trying to soothe? Everybody makes mistakes when they're not at their best; welcome to the experience of being a human. But what matters more to you: Your regrets or your goals? Your past or your future?

If you want to move forward on the path to positivity, investigate the thoughts, feelings, and circumstances that contributed to your mistakes, then choose to forgive yourself by letting go of that story. You'll clear up your mind to find creative solutions and take meaningful action going forward.

Feel Your Feelings

Letting go of self-blame is a process, not a one-time effort. Neuroplasticity gives you the power to create a more positive mind-set over time through daily positive thinking habits.

You may have forgiven yourself for your mistakes in the last section, but don't be surprised if you wake up tomorrow and once again feel remorse. Don't resist! Remember, avoiding your negative emotions is like being stuck in quicksand—the more you try to escape, the deeper you sink.

Instead, feel your feelings and practice PAIN. Remember why you chose to forgive yourself yesterday and what you're doing to take responsibility for creating a better outcome in the future. After several repetitions, your default perspective on this situation will shift.

POSITIVITY IN PRACTICE

This chapter was full of suggestions about sitting with your pain, dealing with discomfort, and committing to taking radical responsibility for living true to your values. These are not always the easiest choices to make, but they are, as I'm sure you've discovered, the most healing and fulfilling choices, and they bring you into a more sustainable version of positivity than you might have ever known before.

Before we move on to the next chapter, I have one more question for you:

How will you celebrate this milestone in a way that aligns with your values? Remember, relishing in joyful celebration will help hardwire the new thoughts and behaviors you've begun developing in this chapter, and if you share your celebration and insights with another person, you'll be contributing to the positive relationships in your life, too.

"Perfectionism is a
twenty-ton shield that we lug
around thinking it will protect
us when, in fact, it's the thing
that's really preventing us
from flight."

—BRENÉ BROWN

CHAPTER FOUR

Taking Action

You might be wondering why I have been calling you my courageous reader. We don't know one another, after all, so how can I make that assumption? Well, because you're here. And as you've seen by now, the path to positivity consistently brings you outside you're comfort zone, and it takes courage to stay loyal to this path.

In this chapter, you'll leverage that courage even more as you take your goals to the next level. You'll learn how to overcome the stumbling blocks that threaten to throw you off course, like fears, uncertainty, perfectionism, and lack of motivation. When you're done, you'll not only feel more positive, but you'll also know, deep down, that you're a champion of courage. Rock on.

EMBRACE IMPERFECTION

"Perfect" was my middle name growing up. I got perfect grades, I was the youngest star in my school play, and I was captain of the cheerleading team. I dated the most popular boy in school, I wore a size zero, and my well-rounded résumé was polished with service trips and community leadership.

Feeling jealous? Don't. Attempts at perfectionism always include one whopping side effect: misery. I always felt anxious because every social encounter included a risk that someone would find out that I was really just a messy nerd plagued by insecurity. I had no real friends because letting people in would require vulnerability and that didn't line up with my perfect image. I maintained my cheerleader body with an eating disorder. I couldn't let other people down, which meant I had to fake a smile and do a lot of things I didn't enjoy doing. I swallowed so many of these perfectionist pills that it contributed to my complete collapse into depression.

Perfectionism is not about excellence; it's about fear. We fear that we'll be rejected, dismissed, disliked, unloved, or unworthy of our goals if we don't get things *just* right. But when we don't control our fears, they control us—driving us into anxiety, inauthenticity, and self-criticism. This is at the heart of Brené Brown's book *The Gifts of Imperfection*. When we embrace our flaws, she argues, we find the courage to overcome paralyzing fears and self-consciousness and become more connected and compassionate toward ourselves and other people.

Perfection Paralysis

There's nothing wrong with striving for high standards, but you know you've moved into perfectionist territory when you're chasing overly demanding, self-imposed standards. According to research documented in 2017 in the journal *Mindfulness*, several kinds of negative cognitive distortions maintain perfectionism, including "all-or-nothing" evaluations of success, self-talk incorporating "shoulds" and "musts," and focusing on the negative while discounting the positive. When you fail to meet your standards, this leads to self-criticism and counterproductive behaviors like list making and overpreparing. Researchers demonstrated that these strategies give you a fleeting sense of control, but ultimately impair your performance, because they drain your energy, take up valuable time, and reaffirm your fear of failure.

This is the perfection paralysis: Striving to be flawless cripples your progress, productivity, and emotional well-being. As Voltaire once wrote, "The best is the enemy of the good."

More Than "Good Enough"

Here's another ironic datapoint about perfectionism: When you *do* meet those dysfunctional standards, rather than relish in your accomplishment, you quickly reappraise those standards as "not being demanding enough." The mountain gets higher and higher, and you never look around to appreciate the view.

It's important to remember that nothing you do is ever beyond criticism. No matter how well you raise your child, how fit you become, or how big you grow your business, somebody will *always* be able to find fault. (And often that somebody is you.) That's okay, though, because overcoming perfectionism doesn't happen by avoiding feedback; it happens by correcting the distorted thinking that got you here in the first place.

What are the standards you set for yourself, personally and professionally? Are they fair, reasonable, and realistic? Do they make you feel confident and cared for? What are the consequences of having those standards? What is an alternative, more helpful standard? (Bonus points if you align your standard with your values.)

When you replace perfectionism with high, yet healthy, standards, you almost always find that you're actually doing a much better job than you think you are.

Practice Over Perfection

After setting better standards, it's important to use positive thinking techniques to empower your forward progress. Avoid all-or-nothing cognitive distortions like "I buckled and snuck a snack in before dinner. I clearly have no willpower." Really? Does one slip-up mean you have zero willpower? Does it negate all of the other experiences in your life where you've successfully employed willpower? Instead of utter failure or complete success, what's a more helpful way of evaluating your progress?

Similarly, if you're a perfectionist, you're more likely to obsess over the one question you got wrong rather than the 30 questions you got right. To counter this negativity bias, commit to a practice of documenting your progress. Know that your brain naturally skims over your successes, and that it's your job to focus at least as much on what's going right as what's going wrong. This sense of consistent progress will make you experience the joy of personal growth and improvement, rather than the consistent angst of falling short.

When working toward your goals, trust this formula:

consistent effort + positive thinking = incredible progress

In other words, repeating habits over and over, while being kind to yourself, learning from your experiences, and celebrating your achievements, will inevitably lead to improvement and excellence.

DO THIS NOW: CONFRONT YOUR FEARS

Fear destroys more dreams than failure. It's not the fear itself that gets in the way, though; it's your relationship to it. Fear can't stop you from quitting your job or getting on an airplane; after all, it's just an experience happening inside your mind and body. Only you can choose how you want to respond to that experience, and when you're working with fear, the only way out is through.

Two types of fears tend to sabotage your progress toward your goals: fears of what you'll have to experience in order to achieve that goal, and fears of what you'll lose or gain when you achieve that goal. In other words, the reason that you don't act in full alignment with your goal is because there's a gap between what you say you want and what you *actually* feel comfortable changing or creating.

With this in mind, get your journal and answer the following questions in order to figure out what fears are inhibiting your progress on the goal you've set for this book.

1. In order to achieve this goal, what discomfort or vulnerability will I have to face?

2. What are the benefits of staying in my comfort zone? What discomfort do I get to avoid?
3. Once I achieve this goal, how will my life change? For example, what new things will I be responsible for? What people will I be around? What expectations will there be of me? How will it affect my time? How will it affect my relationships? How will it affect my income? How do I feel about these changes? Do I trust myself to sustain and maintain them?
4. What will my family think of me when I achieve this goal? What about my friends? My community? The world? My higher power?
5. What will I have to lose or give up in order to achieve this goal?

Identifying your fears is uncomfortable, but now that you know what they are, you have the power to respond to them with wisdom. Using the positive thinking tools you're learning about in this book will help you work with your thoughts, emotions, and behaviors so that you can slowly confront those fears and get back on track with what matters most.

OPENING TO UNCERTAINTY

John was dating Ashley for about six months but hesitated to call her his girlfriend. "I just want to be absolutely sure she's the right choice," he said, "so I'm going to send her several compatibility questionnaires. If all the tests indicate that we're compatible long term and I calculate that we have a 90 percent likelihood of staying together, then I'll make it official."

Perhaps this appeals to you as an extremely "rational" approach to mating, but buried behind John's so-called devotion to logic is his inability to tolerate uncertainty, which causes him excessive anxiety and challenges. When he got a finger wart, John stayed up all night googling the possible causes. He avoids meeting his "hyper-emotional" mother because he doesn't know "exactly what he'd be dealing with." He stayed two years in a job he hated because he preferred to "dance with the devil he knew."

Research from 2012, published in the journal *Behaviour Research and Therapy,* shows that people who can't tolerate uncertainty overestimate the likelihood that negative outcomes will occur, which perpetuates worry and interferes with problem solving and performance. In reality, whether you're trying out a new recipe or navigating a major life transition, success is never a sure thing, so resistance to uncertainty is unhelpful. On the path to positivity, your goal is not to overcome uncertainty, but to make peace with it.

Future Projections

We discussed the benefits of optimism in chapter 2. When you expect good things, not only does it make you feel energized and motivated, it also increases your chances of success. In the face of uncertainty, optimism isn't about expecting everything to go according to plan; rather, it's about embracing what you can't control: "Here's what I know, and here's what I don't know. Even though I don't have all the information, I'm going to move forward and expect good things. If I make a mistake, I'll be able to bounce back, and I'll learn from that experience to do better next time."

This mind-set requires you to stay away from the world of "what ifs," as this obsession with predicting the future is a cognitive distortion that bolsters unhelpful levels of angst. Moreover, if your attention is in the future, then you have fewer mental resources available to skillfully navigate the present moment. John, for example, was so preoccupied with figuring out where he would be with Ashley in 20 years, he wasn't devoting sufficient attention to developing a better relationship with her from day to day.

Many Possibilities

"One goal, many paths." Remembering this mantra is one of the best tools for navigating uncertainty because it keeps you from feeling emotionally dependent on achieving only one outcome. If you want to become a yoga teacher but you're not sure if you'll be able to find a job in that competitive industry, return to your values and your "why" to explore alternative possibilities. Perhaps you're drawn to yoga because you want to help other people become more body positive. How else might you fulfill that desire until your dream job comes through? Could you start a YouTube channel to talk about body positivity? Or create a holistic wellness committee at your current company?

This psychological flexibility doesn't ask you to abandon your pursuit to become a yoga teacher; rather, it helps you deal with the inevitable uncertainty of this journey. You're less likely to relinquish your mission or feel like a failure if you're willing to trade complete control of the outcome for a commitment to the underlying values driving you in that direction.

Be Willing to Accept Failure

Moreover, the more you embrace failure as a step to success, the more likely you are to achieve your goals. Research from Columbia University shows that high school students' science grades improved after they learned about the failures of Einstein and Marie Curie, whereas students who only learned about the scientists' achievements saw their grades decline.

Failure will be a part of every meaningful journey you embark on, so accept this experience as an invitation for reflection. If you don't achieve the outcome you're striving toward, ask yourself what good came from your experience. What strengths, resources, and insights did you gain that will empower you to have a better future?

When it comes to your goal, what kind of uncertainty are you facing? In your journal, write down a list of at least five things that you're unclear about. For example, include small things, like what you'll eat for dinner tonight, as well as bigger questions, like where you'll live one year from now, or where you will be in your career in five years.

Next, reflect on how you behave when these uncertainties arise. What are your favorite strategies for avoiding, ignoring, or otherwise trying to get around these uncertainties? Do you make extensive lists? Seek reassurance from your friend 20 times? Reach for a drink? Procrastinate? Triple or quadruple check your work (and then do it five times more)? Distract your mind with loud music? Remember, don't judge yourself while doing this discovery work. Practice acceptance of your imperfections and negative habits first; change them second.

Then put on your cape and activate your neuroplasticity superpowers. Reflect on the three aspects of your experience and what positive changes you can affect in one or all of them:

1. Thoughts: When these experiences of uncertainty arise in your mind, what positive thoughts can you practice? What will you choose to remember about uncertainty, "failure," resilience, and alternative outcomes?

2. Emotions: You can't feel certain in the face of uncertainty, so what would you like to feel instead? How can you hold both uncertainty and those other positive emotions at the same time?

3. Behaviors: What healthy behaviors can you choose to help you stay present and take action in uncertain

circumstances, rather than avoid them? (Hint: My favorites are deep breaths, laughter, and big hugs.)

After completing the exercise, here's something to keep in mind: Changing your reaction to negative thoughts, feelings, or behaviors is an ongoing practice, not a one-time exercise. Every time you change a cognitive distortion in the midst of uncertain circumstances, take five minutes to journal about the experience and answer the following questions: What was the circumstance? Did you change the thought, the emotion, the behavior, or all three? How did the change(s) impact your experience? What was the most helpful? What impact do these changes have on your ability to achieve your goal? Every time you bring this mindful approach to your change-making efforts, you improve your natural abilities to respond to uncertain experiences with confidence and grace.

EYES ON THE PRIZE

By this point in the book, you've been armed with all the knowledge and tools required to approach your goals with optimism, resilience, and positivity, but you might also be asking yourself, "What the heck am I actually supposed to do now?"

Good question! Let's start by remembering the goal you set in chapter 1. You may have also tweaked this goal in chapter 3 to create alignment with your values. Let's say your goal is to use positive thinking skills to create two close friendships in the next six months. Zoom in to exactly six months from today, when you have successfully established those friendships. What are you doing? What kind of people are you with? What habits do you possess? What qualities do you embody? What have you let go of? What thoughts are you thinking?

Things may not materialize exactly as you envision, but the point is to get clear enough that the path toward the goal becomes transparent.

Make a Plan

Research published in 2002 in the journal *British Journal of Health Psychology* shows that creating a clear action plan makes you three times more likely to achieve your goals. Simply by writing down when and where you intend to implement your intentions makes you more confident, capable, and motivated. As you devise your plan, remember that changing your life through positive neuroplasticity is about developing new habits in your thoughts, emotions, and behaviors. Regular repetition is key.

Following our earlier example, to build a close friendship, you have to spend 200 hours with someone according to research published in the *Journal of Social and Personal Relationships*. Maybe you decide that you will join a choir because members will share your passion for music and it's an easy way to rack up those hours. But don't stop there. Go all the way into the practical and logistical elements of your plan: Find the specific choir you want to join, pay for three months, and put the weekly Sunday rehearsal in your calendar.

Beyond showing up (a behavior), you might also see a need to decrease your social anxiety (thoughts and emotions) in order to open up to people. Set aside time each week to work through and challenge your negative thoughts about why socializing is unsafe or uncomfortable. Balance your negativity bias by practicing the face it, feed it, feel it technique every time you have a positive interaction with other people.

Make It Simple

I once had a client who decided that she was going to do *everything* in her power to lower her inflammation levels. She decided she would eliminate sugar and dairy and have a daily practice of qigong, meditation, turmeric lattes, and eating three cups of greens. After one week, she was so overwhelmed with all these changes that she decided to quit completely.

If you want to achieve your goals, KISS your action plan: Keep It Sweet and Simple. Choose no more than two concrete habits to develop at once. After you've internalized those habits, choose two more.

Taking Action

You know yourself—you've set goals in the past that you've achieved, and others that fell through. Take a few minutes to map out the factors that helped you stay on track when you *did* achieve your goals and the factors that threw you off course when you *didn't*. Then set yourself up for success by incorporating the factors that helped you succeed and create contingency plans to overcome the challenges that threaten to derail you.

The most common pitfall is your conditioned preference for comfort. As we've discussed, change, even when it's "good for you," often feels uncomfortable. On your way to choir practice, your conditioned ways of thinking will come to the surface: "I'm not really in the mood to sing. I'll skip practice today." Review the section in chapter 3 on pushing past discomfort (page 63) to create a plan for overcoming these urges.

The other common pitfall occurs when life throws you a curveball. For example, if you break your ankle, you might not be able to drive to choir practice. In these circumstances, remember your mantra: "one goal, many paths." I recommend that you perform a premortem, in which you list every single thing that could get in the way of executing your plan and then the solutions to continue making progress.

GETTING MOTIVATED

Do you lose motivation when you're thrown too many curveballs or it takes too long to reach your goals? This is a normal reaction to a common situation, but fortunately it's also an obstacle you can overcome by incorporating your natural sources of motivation into your implementation plans.

We're all motivated to fulfill our basic needs and, therefore, to earn money too. But in his book *Drive: The Surprising Truth About What Motivates Us*, Daniel Pink shows that "the best use of money as a motivator is to pay people enough to take the issue of money off the table." In other words, make sure you're earning enough money so that you don't have to constantly be thinking about money. Once you do that, he illustrates, there are three intrinsic motivational factors that lead to better performance and personal satisfaction: autonomy, mastery, and purpose.

Autonomy is our desire to call our own shots and direct our own lives.

Mastery refers to our innate urge to get better at things.

Purpose is our desire to have an impact on other people.

Reflect back on three times in your life when you felt highly motivated. What made you so energized? What about three times when you felt unmotivated and consequently didn't do something you "should" have done. What was missing? The answers to these questions will reveal which of the three motivational sources is most energizing for you. Build them into your goals and action plans to empower yourself with consistent motivation.

YOUR WISE MIND

We've been talking a lot about pursuing your goals by creating new habits in your thoughts, emotions, and behaviors. But don't let all this emphasis on progressing toward the future trigger a sense that the person you are today is somehow not enough. Would you tell your friends who recently had a baby that you can't wait until she grows up and becomes "enough"? Absolutely not. You're excited to see how the child develops, but at the same time, you enjoy how this child is right now. This is the attitude to cultivate toward your own personal development, too. (Remember positive thinking rule number three from chapter 1: Talk to yourself the way you talk to your best friend.)

Accepting Yourself

One of the areas where we tend to turn on ourselves is when we're struggling with doubt, hesitation, and indecision. For the last year, for example, I've had a growing desire to move out of the city onto a farm. My heart jumps at this idea, but my brain tells me it's illogical. "Shut up, emotions! You're being so unreasonable!" Or, "Shut up, brain! Just because it will be difficult doesn't mean it's a bad idea!"

This kind of negative self-talk toward your thoughts, emotions, and confusion is a form of resistance, which you know by now never helps you feel confident or cared for and therefore is not part of your path to positivity. Instead, it's important to accept every aspect of your experience and remind yourself that feeling confused or conflicted is a natural part of life.

What situations stir confusion between your heart and head? Do you try to reject one in favor of the other? Once you practice acceptance, you can tap into what psychologist Marsha Linehan calls your Wise Mind: the place where your thoughts, emotions, experiences, and bodily intuition come together to form an approach to thinking and reacting that balances emotions with reason. Overly emotional thinking can cloud our judgment by being too reactive, yielding impulsive decisions, whereas overly reasonable thinking can cloud our judgment by being too measured, yielding decisions that lack passion. Wise Mind is a combination of the two and encourages us to approach experiences from a "middle path."

As you learn to utilize the Wise Mind perspective, observe all of these aspects of your experience without judgment and ask yourself the following: "What do I know is true? What's even truer than that?" Keep going until you arrive at an insight that feels intuitively right. You'll know you've hit it because it will feel different in your body: grounding and peaceful, yet also uplifting.

Your Achievements Aren't Magic

A crucial part of tapping into your Wise Mind is looking to your own past. Jasmine, a former client of mine, had been diagnosed with diabetes and had to change her whole diet in order to save her life. She asked, "How am I ever going to do this? I don't even know where to start. I'm so addicted to carbs, I just don't think I'll ever be able to get off of them."

I asked Jasmine to reflect on the times she had succeeded making changes in the past. She recounted stories of having to make new friends every year as a child because her parents moved around a lot, and how she had to downsize her whole life during the recession when she lost her job. We reflected on how strong and resilient these accomplishments proved she was, and how she could tap into the very same strengths and social support she did in the past in order to achieve her new wellness goals.

Similarly, your achievements aren't magic—you've worked hard to get where you are today. In the past, the negativity bias may have made you dismiss your successes as trivial, but that doesn't erase them from your memory. If you're feeling confused, look back at how you navigated similar circumstances in the past. The wisdom of your own experience awaits.

You Can't Be Right All the Time

My client David often confused the Wise Mind with the popular understanding of intuition: his gut feelings. He'd get an impulsive instinct about something and immediately act on it. This often misguided him because his gut instinct wasn't led by the deeper, slower, and reflective process I described previously but rather by an automatic reaction conditioned by his past. Similarly, if you're in an extremely emotional or exhausted state, it's difficult to investigate your experience with an open and curious mind. That's why you have to take a step back from the emotions of an experience. This "self-distancing," as psychologists call it, is crucial for cultivating your Wise Mind.

A part of positive thinking means fully accepting the fact that things won't feel 100 percent clear all the time and realizing that you can never have all the information. When you're committed to learning from your mistakes, rather than judging them, and working with the aspects of your experience that are within your control, then you can rest knowing that you're on the right path and be satisfied with where you are in the present moment.

Don't Apologize (Unless You've Hurt Someone)

*"But what if I make the wrong decision
and hurt someone I love?"*

This is another common block to trusting our own Wise Mind. My client Tyler, for example, wanted to go back to school at age 40 to become a psychologist, but he was afraid he might not be able to make his new career successful and that his wife and kids would suffer. We discussed how Tyler could approach his transition in the wisest way, based on his accomplishments in the past and advice from others who had made a similar transition. But ultimately, we agreed that this transition would involve uncertainty and mistakes that would affect both his life and his family's.

Rather than apologize for who he was or what he was working toward, Tyler realized that it was much more helpful to thank his family for their support. He also encouraged his wife and daughter to make the choices that were most aligned with their values, so that every individual in the family was fulfilled and could support one another.

Don't apologize for being a human, either. If your mistakes caused hurt to another person or yourself, acknowledge that pain. It's helpful to explain the thoughts, feelings, and circumstances that led to your mistake and your intentions to do better in the future. Then move on, feeling proud that you're growing wiser every day.

UNBURDEN YOURSELF

We carry all kinds of fears around our necks (recall the exercise on identifying your fears from earlier in the chapter). And yet, believe it or not, fear is a natural and intelligent emotion. It knocks on your door when there's an important message you need to hear, like the punch in your gut that screams "Get out of the street, a car is coming!"

The problem is that fear triggers the stress response in your body, which brings up a lot of discomfort, so your automatic instinct is to rid yourself of that discomfort as fast as possible by fighting with or fleeing from whatever is inciting your fear. For example, when you're about to speak at a meeting, fear might whisper, "Don't screw this up or everybody will laugh at you." It might seem like fear's message is to retreat. However, that choice would only make your fear of public speaking more daunting the next time. Because avoidance won't solve the problem, fear has a deeper message: You're letting negative thinking steer your mind's ship. When you hand over the wheel to positive thinking, you can learn how to let your fears go.

Making and Learning from Mistakes

One of our greatest fears is making mistakes because we believe the horror story in our head. When I submitted the manuscript for this book to my editor for the first time, I felt scared about getting her feedback because I knew she'd be pointing out all my mistakes. I began observing my thoughts, which were saying, "If you made too many mistakes, the publisher will probably drop you. You'll have to tell your friends you lost your book deal. You'll have to deal with the disappointment of letting yourself down." These kinds of thoughts are at the heart of most of our fears: We believe, incorrectly, that the consequences will be dramatic and that we won't be able to cope.

I accepted my fears, appreciative that they pointed me toward the negative thoughts I was allowing to taint my mood and behavior. Then I challenged the thoughts behind them: Were these predictions really accurate? No. Were there other ways I could handle my mistakes? Yes. Was I resilient enough to learn and grow from my mistakes? Absolutely.

When I received my editor's feedback, she did, in fact, point out many mistakes in my writing. However, I was already mentally prepared, because I had been practicing new thoughts, which reminded me that I was lucky to have a mentor helping me achieve my goals and that I was capable of learning from my mistakes. By rearranging my thoughts, I was able to calmly integrate her feedback and muster the courage to try again.

What mistakes are you worried about making in relation to the goal you set for this book? How can you use positive thinking to overcome this fear? Can you accept that mistakes are a necessary part of progress? Look for the lessons you learned and commit to making improvements. Practice gratitude for how the experience has helped you grow. Remember your resilience. These are the keys to reducing the grip of fear around making mistakes.

Gracefully Accept Feedback

Research published in 2007 in the *Review of Educational Research* shows that feedback is one of the most powerful influences on learning and achievement. And now that you have the tools to navigate and learn from your mistakes, you're capable of asking for feedback. The key to extracting meaningful growth from these vulnerable experiences is to listen with an open curiosity. Ask clarifying questions and summarize what you hear. No matter what you're feeling, respond with: "Thanks! Let me take a little time to process this and get back to you."

Don't take everything you've heard at face value. Instead, consult your Wise Mind. What are your thoughts saying? What are your emotions saying? Have you gotten this feedback before? How can learning from this feedback help you achieve your goals? What are your values, and how can they guide your response?

Once you've figured out what's true and helpful for you, take corrective action. And here's a pro tip: Share your plan of action with the person who gave you feedback. Leadership consultant Jennifer Porter states that this will not only help you learn, but it will also improve your relationship because the other person will know what to expect and can see that their conversations with you had an impact.

Trust Yourself

The key to letting go of your fears is trusting yourself. I can't promise that you'll never make that mistake again, but I *can* assure you that if you use the positive thinking tools in this book, you'll be able to handle any challenging experience and move forward in your personal development. To do this, let yourself trust the evidence-based power of positive thinking; you can trust your willingness to try again and your ability to learn and grow from failure. You can trust your values in order to derive meaning from this experience. And, finally, you can trust your Wise Mind and your incredible resilience, my courageous reader.

POSITIVITY IN PRACTICE

By now you have a clear implementation plan of action to achieve your goals, and you know how to overcome the most common pitfalls on the journey: perfectionism, uncertainty, lack of motivation, confusion, and fear. The key with all of these challenges is to remember that trying to run away from your negativity is like trying to escape from your shadow: You can try to run away all you want, but you'll never be successful and you'll waste a lot of energy. Instead, you can leverage every ounce of negative experiences for courage, growth, and self-awareness.

Hopefully, you've also realized that this path is about so much more than achieving your goals; it's about creating, experience by experience, the masterpiece that is you. You find positivity not by achieving every desire you've ever had or optimizing every moment of your life, but by realizing who you are on the deepest level: a Wise Mind, rooted in important values, learning and growing from every experience, cultivating the thoughts, emotions, and behaviors that support you along the way.

Up to this point, what have you learned about who you really are beyond your goals, beyond your imperfections, and beyond your mistakes and confusion? What lies beneath all that? What about yourself do you trust, no matter what?

"Self-care is never a selfish act—it is simply good stewardship of the only gift I have, the gift I was put on earth to offer to others."

—PARKER PALMER

CHAPTER FIVE

Nurturing Positivity

The path to positivity is a marathon, not a sprint. This doesn't mean that you can't create positive new habits quickly or that it will take you a long time to achieve your goals; in fact, I'm confident you've *already* created meaningful breakthroughs with the practices you've done to reshape your perspective, emotions, and actions in the previous chapters. But as you continue to grow, you'll consistently be faced with new circumstances and challenges and you'll need energy and support to maintain your positive thinking practice.

This chapter gives you the skills and science to persevere. You'll learn how to create the outer lifestyle and relationships that nurture all the inner work you're doing, including developing or maintaining techniques for self-care, establishing healthy boundaries, and engaging in compassionate exercises that improve your resilience in working with your inner and outer worlds. And perhaps, most importantly, you'll learn to practice positivity in the context of the most important relationship you'll ever have: the one with yourself.

REFILL YOUR RESERVOIR

Positive thinking gives you energy: Optimists live longer, healthier lives, and encouraging self-talk motivates you to pursue your goals. However, you also have to *give* energy to positive thinking. It requires discipline and hard work to build new mental habits. That's where self-care comes in—it's your way of setting yourself up for success by making sure you always have fuel for your positivity tank.

The most effective guidance for self-care is a provocative inversion of the classic "golden rule": Treat yourself the way you want your loving partner to treat you. When you fantasize about what you crave in relationships, you allow yourself to develop a substantive definition for self-care. Your ideal spouse listens enthusiastically to your ideas, stands up for your needs, cooks nice meals for you, helps you grow, laughs at your idiosyncrasies, and loves you unconditionally. Self-care means approaching yourself with the same warmth, respect, and kindness.

Self-Care Is Not Selfish

People often confuse self-care with self-indulgence. Champagne and massages, for example, fall into the latter category; these are the special things you do for yourself in the name of pleasure and pampering. Self-care is more practical. It's a daily discipline of making the choices that contribute to your wellness. The goal is to nourish your positive energy by making time for things that help you and keeping out the things that drain you. What do you read, eat, and drink every day, and how do they affect your energy? How much sleep do you commit to? Whose opinions do you let in? How many hours do you allow yourself on social media?

Ethan, a former client of mine, was hustling around the clock to get his business off the ground, but he was exhausted and overworked. He was getting sick more often and he needed a little more coffee every day just to make it through, both of which inhibited his ability to think positively or even work with his thoughts. When I asked him what he was doing to take care of his mind and body, he protested, "All this me, me, me is uncomfortable. It's not about what I need. My focus is on my family and my business." Then I asked Ethan to imagine how he would be different toward his family and business if he practiced self-care for a week. "I'd be a lot more energized," he said. "I'd feel better about myself, more positive, and more excited to go to work in the morning and come home in the evening because I'd actually have the energy to enjoy and engage the things I'm doing."

"And which version of Ethan do you think your colleague and family would prefer? The frustrated, exhausted one sitting in front of me, or the energized, positive one you just described?" I asked. That's when it clicked for Ethan. Self-care isn't selfish; in fact, it empowers you to bring more positivity into your relationships.

Know Your Boundaries

Are you always trying to please other people? Do you often say yes when you really mean no? Especially if you value kindness, collaboration, and service, "yes" often becomes your automatic response, before you have time to think through the repercussions of your commitment. However, when you say yes to everyone else, you usually end up spending more time helping other people fulfill their goals and values than realizing your own. This often leads to exhaustion, regret, and even resentment: *Why am I everyone's doormat? Why does everyone expect so much from me? Why am I always the one people come too?*

Saying no also elicits discomfort about disappointing someone or relinquishing their approval. *You're not a good [parent/spouse/friend/colleague] if you don't do this.* What's critical is to keep the big picture in mind. Sure, immediately saying yes is the easiest option, but how will this obligation affect your well-being and relationship a few hours, days, or months from now? If you know that yes will brew long-term resentment, then you can say no from a positive place, knowing your intentions are good. Communicating why your no comes from a concerned and compassionate place is also helpful to diminish your discomfort.

It's Okay to Get Tired

When you're motivated to achieve your goals, you always wish there were more hours in the day or that you had more energy to give. But at some point, you will hit your limit. Putting in your all and working with your thoughts will make you tired from time to time. This is perfectly normal, but it's also an invitation to examine your boundaries and see what's draining your energy.

My client Alana felt perpetually exhausted. She had three kids and worked full time, so she assumed that fatigue was unavoidable. When we took a hard look at her life, though, Alana realized she had no boundaries with her TV or phone, which meant she rarely got the eight hours of sleep she needed. Moreover, Alana often attended social engagements she wasn't interested in and did things for her kids that they could easily do for themselves. Alana decided to create appropriate boundaries as an act of self-care, and with time she felt much better.

"I've noticed that my kids are more affected by my overall energy than by whether or not I give in to every single one of their requests," she said. And she's right: Positive boundaries are about learning to love yourself and others better.

DO THIS NOW: SET POSITIVE BOUNDARIES

Even if you've bought in to the concept of setting boundaries as an act of self-care, it's easy to get tripped up in the implementation. For example, raise your hand if you've ever uttered something like, "Well, I want to create a boundary, but . . .
- I don't know how to say no."
- I don't want her to think I don't like her."
- I'm worried I'll ruffle too many feathers."

Not to worry! Next is an effective formula for compassionately asserting your boundaries. Before you dive in, get clear on what boundaries you need to set. Think about where you struggle the most to maintain your energy and positivity. What are the things, people, places, activities, and thought patterns that—if they could be magically eliminated or changed—would make it easier for you to feel positive and energetic?

Choose one concrete boundary you'd like to set with another person and follow this format to express your decision:

1. Acknowledge the boundary issue:

   Hey, boss, I know you're used to me responding to emails up to 11 p.m.

2. Discuss your role in establishing the boundary issue, and how it has transformed into a new norm for the relationship:

   I acknowledge that I set this precedent, because I wanted you to know how committed I am to this job.

3. In clear language, express how the boundary issue is impacting you:

   The problem is that all that screen time late at night is making it difficult to fall asleep. So, I'm coming into work exhausted, rather than refreshed, and I'm not able to do as good of a job as I want to.

4. Set your boundary as a solution to the problem:

   So, in order to be a better overall employee, I'm going to turn off my phone after 7 p.m. I'm really confident that this will make me more productive overall and positively affect my relationship with our customers.

5. Accept and discuss the other person's concerns:

   I know you might be worried that this will affect the customer response rate, so let's discuss how we can work through this obstacle. Here are a few ideas I have . . .

6. Reinforce your commitment to your boundary:

   Thanks for working with me on this. I know it will involve some changes in our communication, but I'm committed to making this change because I know for sure it's critical to my long-term well-being and my performance in this company.

LOOKING INWARD

Positivity is an inside job. Whenever you're facing challenges on the road to your dreams, the most positive, helpful response always begins with looking inward to examine what baggage you're bringing to the experience and how you can work with your thoughts, emotions, and behaviors to create a better one. Warning: This is rarely your automatic instinct, because as humans, we are conditioned to try to change things outside of ourselves before looking at the architecture of our inner world. That's why it's critical to cultivate the habits of mindfulness, meditation, and self-compassion: These practices train your brain to be present with your inner experience.

Mindfulness

Mindfulness is a nonjudgmental way to better understand your experiences through curiosity, openness, and acceptance. You've already begun cultivating mindfulness through PAIN and Wise Mind practices by learning to observe your experience without trying to change it. But it isn't easy to activate an accepting mind-set, especially when you're feeling triggered. Your brain's amygdala is in the driver's seat, which is like your inner NASCAR driver who runs on adrenaline and reacts with a fight, a flight, or a freeze response. You can't practice mindfulness until you hand the wheel over to your prefrontal cortex, which is like your inner GPS system: When you hit a roadblock, she doesn't curse or blame another driver; rather, she looks at all the information of that present moment and gently, intelligently reroutes.

The key to activating your prefrontal cortex is relaxation. There are many ways to relax, including deep belly breathing, yoga, progressive muscle relaxation, and earthing. Choose your favorite strategy and keep going until your breath returns to normal and your muscles loosen. Then begin your mindfulness practice by consciously play-acting a new identity, one that allows you to "self-distance" from your experience. You're no longer a lawyer trying to win your case; you're the judge, objectively reviewing all the evidence in front of you. As you observe your experience, pay attention to your thoughts, feelings, and sensations, without analyzing them. Imagine every thought and feeling is a different lawyer with different information, and your job is to impartially listen to every angle of your experience. You'll make your verdict later.

Meditation

Meditation is a focused, one-pointed concentration of all your attention on one particular thing: a thought, a breath, or a music track, for example. I like to joke that I've been meditating all my life, but for the first 21 years, I was meditating on the wrong things: my negative thoughts. "Stupid, stupid, stupid, stupid," I'd say to myself all day. This focus was accidental, though, so we can't really call it meditation, but it's a common experience in that we tend to run the same thoughts through our mind until we consciously work to understand and change them.

My teacher Sally Kempton calls meditation "the unconditional embrace of the fullness of your experience." She's referring to a more deliberate form of focusing, and one that helps you cultivate positivity. In meditation, you're fully awake and alert, and it may be helpful to close your eyes to improve your capacity to focus. Then use the power of your concentration to stay focused on one thing, such as your thoughts, emotions, or bodily sensations. The goal is not to let your mind cling, but to just observe as whatever you're focusing on naturally changes. You want to remain present, and whenever you get distracted or sucked into a thought, you return back to your point of focus.

The more you meditate, the more you'll naturally respond to your experiences with mindfulness. In *Altered Traits: Science*

Reveals How Meditation Changes Your Mind, Brain, and Body,
authors Daniel Goleman and Richard Davidson use the latest
research in neuroscience to demonstrate that mindfulness practices dull activity in our amygdala and increase the connections
between the amygdala and prefrontal cortex, not just temporar-
ily, but permanently. Long-term meditators, therefore, perceive
situations as less stressful because they've trained their brains to
think slowly and objectivity.

Self-Compassion

Beneficial as mindfulness is, it requires tremendous courage
to be present with your anger, fear, and failures. A 2014 article
in *Science* magazine discussed the results of a shocking study
completed by researcher Timothy Wilson and his colleagues, in
which they demonstrated that people preferred to give themselves a painful electric shock instead of sitting quietly with their
thoughts! But knowing mindfulness is the way to wisdom and
positivity, you can create the courage to stay present through
practicing self-compassion, that is treating yourself with kindness and understanding.

According to pioneering self-compassion researcher Kristen
Neff, there are three crucial ingredients to self-compassion. First,
acknowledge your vulnerability. *"Hey love,"* you might whisper
inwardly, *"I really care about this pain."* Second, remember that
stress is a part of life and that you're not alone. You can think
of people who've been where you are and take refuge in that
solidarity. Finally, offer yourself a kind message, like *"I'm doing
the best I can"* or *"Making a bad decision doesn't make me a
bad person."* In an article in 2007 in the *Journal of Research
in Personality*, Neff and her colleagues shared the results of
two studies in which practicing self-compassion in this way
decreased people's anxiety and improved their well-being. This

improved mental state strengthens your capacity to practice mindfulness and judiciously respond to your experience.

When we visualize, we use our imagination and our senses to bring to life the experiences in our mind. Research shows that the brain doesn't differentiate between a real memory and a visualized one. A 1995 study published in the *Journal of Neurophysiology,* for example, showed that the experience in the brains of people who visualized playing the piano and those who actually played the piano were the same. In other words, when you imagine something vividly, your brain chemistry changes as though the experience was real and your mind records it as a real memory. Therefore, you can develop and reinforce the positivity skills you are learning in this book, such as living in line with your values embracing failure, practicing self-care, or welcoming self-compassion, by visualizing them.

Next is a self-compassion visualization exercise. Read through the directions entirely first. Once you understand how to visualize, go through the entire practice with your eyes closed.

1. Visualize yourself in a healing space, real or imaginary: a space that brings you a sense of serenity or joy. Now notice the shapes and colors you see, breathe in the fragrance of the place, feel the air and the energy around you, notice the sounds or the silence of this place, and really allow yourself to settle in.

2. Once you're feeling relaxed, think about a situation that's bringing up some difficult feelings for you. Reflect on the thoughts you're having about this experience. Why is it so bad? How are you judging yourself or others? What's it like for you to be living inside these thoughts and emotions?

3. Bring your awareness back to the healing space around you. Imagine that, in front of you, there appears a person or figure that represents the embodiment of unconditional compassion and wisdom. Imagine looking into the eyes of this figure and feel as they gaze at you with unconditional love, understanding, and acceptance. Then listen as this compassionate being offers you a kind or caring message.

4. Now turn this wisdom into a positive message toward yourself. If, for example, the figure tells you, "Your best is always good enough," convert these words into "My best is always good enough," and repeat this statement, this mantra, several times.

5. Now return to your visualized healing space and imagine a door opening where other people who have struggled with the same feelings you're struggling with begin to enter. Maybe you know them or maybe they are strangers, but just watch as you are joined in solidarity with others who share the same fears, regrets, disappointments, or losses you're dealing with. See and feel that you are not alone. Offer your kind positive message to these people, allowing it to comfort them, too.

INCREASING SELF-ESTEEM

When Claudia tried this self-compassion exercise for the first time, she became extremely uncomfortable. "I haven't achieved my goals, I'm lazy, and I'm fat. Why should I be nice to myself?" she said. If you felt similar resistance, then, like most, you might struggle with low self-esteem.

Self-esteem is different from self-confidence. Self-confidence is about trusting yourself and your ability to succeed in the world; self-esteem is your appraisal of your own worth. A healthy self-esteem is not arrogance or conceitedness. Rather, it's about believing that you're as worthy of respect, love, and security as much as anybody else.

When you have low self-esteem, it comes with a vicious inner voice, one that says you don't deserve the things you want, blames you for everything, constantly reminds you of your failures, and negatively compares you to others. This negative self-perception makes the path to positivity extremely challenging. How can you build a positive outer life on a negative inner foundation? Research from 2019 in the academic journal *Psychiatry Investigation* shows that people with low self-esteem are more self-conscious and struggle with psychological adjustment. They also tend to suppress positive emotions, have increased negative emotions, and exhibit many depressive behaviors. This means that if you struggle with low self-esteem, you'll take fewer risks and shy away from valuable experiences like authentic self-expression, asking for help, taking leadership positions, and proactive problem solving.

The good news is that you can improve your self-esteem by changing your inner voice. That voice was created and strengthened over time by your habitual thoughts and feelings, and, as you know by now, you have the power to change these things over time. This starts with building your self-awareness and practicing self-acceptance.

Getting to Like Yourself

Because of the work you've put in throughout the last several chapters, you've already got the self-awareness ball rolling. But let's dive deeper to uncover your strengths. What have you been naturally good at ever since you were young? With what kinds of tasks or problems do people consistently ask you for help? What do you often receive compliments about? Which activities can you do for hours without getting tired? If you've ever taken the Myers-Briggs personality test, what is your personality type?

What are your strengths? Notice the qualities that keep coming up, as these are your core strengths.

Perhaps your inner critic popped in while you were answering these questions, saying, "Lame. I wish you had X, Y, and Z strengths instead," or "Everyone is good at this . . . it's nothing special." If so, here's your opportunity to change those negative thoughts by practicing self-acceptance. The truth is, your strengths are important: They serve you and others, and they make the world a better place. To drive home self-acceptance, complete the following statement for each of your core strengths:

(My strength) is such a valuable skill/trait because it helps (person/organization/community) to (result).

Here are two examples to get you started:

My compassion is such a valuable skill/trait because it helps my partner feel loved and heard.

My perseverance is such a valuable skill/trait because it helps my neighborhood stay safe for our children and families.

Be a Tourist

Accepting your strengths is not enough, though. You must accept your weaknesses, too. Thanks to the negativity bias, you don't need to do much digging to identify your weaknesses. But you'll probably have to work a little harder to accept these parts of yourself. One of the most effective techniques to help nurture self-acceptance with your weaknesses is seeing yourself from a stranger's perspective. Imagine that you're a tourist traveling through your life, watching it unfold from your birth until the present moment. This tourist has no baggage. They don't have any expectations of who you should be. How would they describe your overall life story? How would you describe your personality, your strengths, and your weaknesses?

When witnessed from a stranger's perspective, your life looks a lot more positive because your inner critic isn't influencing your judgment. You probably noticed that the tourist saw more good things than bad about you and that your weaknesses are not damnable qualities but rather normal, acceptable foibles common in many human beings.

Update Your Self-Image

Like every other positive thinking skill we've practiced, raising your self-esteem is a habit. You have to change the way you see yourself and value yourself by thinking differently every day. Research from the *Journal of Personality* suggests that simply writing about important chapters in your life story increases self-esteem, as does deliberately imagining positive memories of yourself (according to another study from *Cognitive Behavioral Therapy*).

Every night before you go to bed, try asking yourself these questions: What are my core values, and how did I honor them? What are my strengths, and how did I use them in meaningful ways? What weaknesses or mistakes came up, and how can I practice self-compassion to help me navigate these vulnerabilities?

THE HIERARCHY OF NEEDS

Maslow's hierarchy of needs, published in 1943, is still among the most popular psychology concepts. In this theory, people have five levels of needs, which we pursue in order: physiological (air, food, water, sleep), safety (shelter, money, employment, health), love (friendship, family, connection), esteem (self-esteem, status, recognition), and self-actualization (living up to one's potential).

Recent research from *The American Journal of Psychology* suggests that although people *do* tend to achieve physiological and safety needs first, the greatest gains in positive feelings result from experiences of love, esteem, and self-actualization. Furthermore, optimal well-being results from a balanced pursuit of all five categories of needs simultaneously.

If you're struggling to make progress on the path to positivity, these insights can help you diagnose the problem. If all of your goals are focused on making more money, for example, and that erodes your time with friends and family, your overall positivity may suffer. Moreover, even if you're struggling financially, you can still feel positive by living true to your values (self-actualization), building your self-esteem, and hanging out with people who make you feel like you belong. Regardless of your circumstances, you always have the power to improve your well-being by improving any one of these five needs.

LOOKING OUTWARD

The Harvard Study of Adult Development, one of the longest-running studies on human well-being, found that the most important factor for long-term happiness, fulfillment, and health is strong, meaningful personal relationships. People who are socially integrated and who have supportive relationships with others have better mental health and higher levels of well-being.

This means more than money, fame, social class, and IQ—the most helpful resources you can cultivate to sustain your path of positivity are positive relationships. Meaningful connections with other people create mental and emotional stimulation and give you the opportunity for self-expression, which is an automatic mood booster. Perhaps more important, these deep relationships also protect you from life's discontents. A good friend or family member provides a safe space to talk about your challenges, offers comfort and reassurance, and even helps you problem solve.

Kindness

It's not the number of friends you have that influences your well-being but rather the quality and satisfaction of your relationships. The two most important pillars for building these meaningful relationships are kindness and gratitude.

Kindness means acting in a way that is benevolent and helpful for the other person. It only creates positivity, however, when your kindness is motivated by the desire to genuinely help the other person, not to gain a reward or to avoid punishment (that's manipulation). Every experience, you'll recall, is built by three things: your thoughts, emotions, and actions. Being nice to someone while harboring inner resentment will not make you more positive; in fact, this kind of inauthenticity creates stress, resentment, and disconnection.

Accordingly, kindness involves inner work. Studies show that people are more kind when they have the skills to take perspective on a situation and regulate their thoughts and emotions.

Gratitude

Similarly, gratitude is about more than saying thanks; it's a profound experience of feeling and sharing appreciation. The key is communicating how the other person enabled value in your life or the positive emotions they made you feel. Not only does this make the other person feel valued and proud, but it also makes them feel more positive toward you and more comfortable expressing concerns within your relationship.

Both gratitude and kindness motivate a continuous cycle of positive behaviors that build intimacy and deep connection in your relationships over time. For example, if someone sends you a letter thanking you for your work, you're likely to want to do something again for that person. Or if someone does something kind for you, you'll feel inclined to reciprocate. The more this cycle continues, the more meaningful the relationship becomes. Research shows that you also receive personal benefits from these prosocial behaviors. Simply by writing down what you're grateful for, for example, you feel happier. In an article published in 2009 in the *Journal of Writing Research*, researchers illustrated that writing these letters in an expressive way cultivates well-being, and just three experiences of 10 to 15 minutes of writing was sufficient to usher in positive change.

Belonging

The fastest way to become a more kind and grateful person is by surrounding yourself with other kind and grateful people. Because we're wired as social beings, who you spend your time with, both personally and professionally, has a fast and powerful impact on how you behave. Once again, though, it's not just about being around these kinds of positive people and communities; it's about creating a meaningful sense of connection and belonging within them.

To cultivate the feeling of belonging, show genuine interest in other people. Celebrate their accomplishments, ask about their passions, values, fears, and hopes, and share yours, too. Take initiative and create opportunities for shared adventure, play, inspiration, and discovery. Most important, be authentic—interact in ways you genuinely enjoy, express the truth of who you are, and set boundaries when you need to.

Finally, make sure you *savor* these experiences of connection and belonging by practicing the face it, feed it, feel it technique. When you have a pleasant experience, like a moment of meaningful connection, enrich that experience by reflecting on it for 30 seconds and then absorb that interaction; imagining it sinking into your body and becoming part of your identity.

DO THIS NOW: IMPROVE YOUR GRATITUDE WITH MINDFULNESS

Gratitude is good for your mental health, for your relationships, and for humanity as a whole. However, we rarely give our positive experiences the attention they need in order to cultivate the thoughts, emotions, and behavior that create the experience of gratitude. Powered by mindfulness, though, you can build your capacity to connect to gratitude each day. The following exercise is adapted from Mindful.org.

This is a full-day exercise, so carry your journal along with you and be aware of every time you say thank you, to everyone from your coffee barista to your mom. Pause and notice the details of this experience:

1. What does it feel like? Is it heartfelt or a habituated social courtesy?
2. What thoughts is it bringing up, if any? Perhaps genuine thoughts of appreciation, or plans for reciprocating the favor, or wondering why you're thanking this person in the first place.
3. What is your body like? Are you facing the other person, making eye contact, and offering an appreciative gesture? Or are you halfway out the door, onto your next interaction?

After this exercise, you will probably realize that your habitual way of saying thank you isn't particularly mindful, but rather absent-minded and absent-hearted. Bringing mindfulness and intention into your gratitude practice going forward requires you to pause when your instinct to say thanks arises. Stop for a moment to name what you feel grateful for. Notice and feel the emotions that these thoughts bring up. *Then* say thank you.

DON'T FORCE IT

We began this book by discussing the importance of creating habits so that you can make lasting changes to your mind-set and life. Let's circle back and end on the same note.

As you've no doubt experienced by now, change doesn't happen overnight, and it takes time to accomplish your goals. When you find yourself having the same argument with your partner for the hundredth time, you might stop to practice PAIN to work through your anger, or dialogue with your negative thinking so you can identify the cognitive distortions that make you lose your cool. But if your partner triggers you again the next day, you'll still be tempted to react with your old argumentative ways because that's still your most practiced, most habitual way of responding. You'll have to do the inner work again and again and again until you finally break through to create new patterns. It *will* happen eventually, but you can't force it.

That's why the most important choice you can make right now is to enjoy your daily practice of positive thinking, rather than treating it like an annoying exercise on the way to your lofty goals. It's a privilege to be able to create and change the way you experience life, not an obligation. So every single time you're mindful enough to stop and work with your thoughts, emotions, and behaviors in a way that aligns with your values, let that be enough for you in that moment. With daily action, not force, change becomes within your grasp.

You Don't Need to Lie to Yourself

Bill Gates once famously said, "Most people overestimate what they can do in one year and underestimate what they can do in 10 years." I couldn't agree more, which is why patience is the key to sustainable progress—you must be able to keep going, even if it's taking longer than you'd hoped. Patience involves a courageous acceptance of your inner and outer reality, the absence of resentment and restlessness, and the retention of hope. What kind of positive thoughts based on optimism, reliance, and compassion can you practice to embrace a patient attitude to your success?

If you're in a bad mood, don't try to trick yourself into a positive attitude. Instead, acknowledge your feelings of unease and your anxiety to "get on with it" and address them with gentle compassion. This shifts you out of drama and into presence, which allows you to anchor in your deeper values and wisdom. Once you connect to that inner clarity, honor what matters most in the present moment by the way you treat yourself and others. This is what makes waiting a bearable, and even enjoyable, experience.

It Will Happen in Time

Instead of asking, "Are we there yet?" trust in the power of the evidence-based habits you've learned in this book. If you go surfing every day, you *will* get better at riding the waves. A changing tide or an aging body may inhibit your progress from time to time, but you *will* become a more skillful surfer. The same is true for all of your goals.

I've been on the path to positivity for over a decade now, and I *still* struggle with negativity. The difference from my past is how today I work through my negative thoughts and feelings quickly and with integrity, rather than spiraling into an argument or letting it affect my self-worth. Similarly, you'll create a more courageous, kind, and resilient mind-set as you continue to practice the positive thinking skills in this book; neuroplasticity proves that this progress is inevitable. This doesn't mean you'll never slip into negativity, just that it will happen less and less frequently, and you'll be much more equipped to deal with it.

Get Support

Remember, close relationships are an asset on your path to positivity. Working with a coach, a therapist, or an accountability partner will help you stay on track and make this experience more joyful and meaningful. Even something as simple as sharing your positive thinking commitments with a friend will catapult your results. Choose someone who can provide support and accountability and follow up with updates on your weekly progress. Do not choose someone who doesn't value positivity, as that could introduce doubt into your practice.

In addition to cultivating a supportive network, use boundary setting to express your needs for support or space from anyone who disapproves of the positivity you're working toward. Your inner critic is enough to handle; you don't need any others.

Now that we're nearing the end of this book, it's time to once again assess your positivity.

Please score each item from 1 to 10, with 10 being the best, based on how true it is for you. Then calculate your positivity score by adding your responses. As you're scoring, remember this is an assessment, not a judgment. You're assessing yourself simply because it helps you focus your efforts going forward. Learning and growing are experiences that bring us great joy and satisfaction, and the results of this assessment will help you know what, specifically, will help you grow even more in the future.

1. I like myself, appreciate my strengths, and accept my imperfections.
2. My daily life and goals are very fulfilling because they are aligned with my core values.
3. I take radical responsibility for my relationship to my experiences by working with my thoughts, emotions, and behaviors.
4. I turn positive experiences into long-term resources. When good things happen, I proactively take time to appreciate, nourish, enrich, and share these experiences.
5. I surround myself with people who believe in kindness, gratitude, and positivity, and I cultivate deep, meaningful relationships with these people.
6. When I experience negative emotions, I pause before reacting and meet my thoughts and feelings with curiosity, compassion, and self-care.
7. I never avoid discomfort or uncertainty; I know I am resilient enough to overcome whatever circumstances I encounter.
8. When I feel lost or confused, I tap into the intuitive intelligence of my Wise Mind and honor its guidance.

9. When I fail, I always look for the growth and learning in my experience, and then continue to move forward toward my goals.

10. On a day-to-day basis, I expect good things, and I feel optimistic about my life.

My positivity score: _____ /100%

Whether your score has increased by 5 points or 50 points, celebrate your progress and enrich the positive emotions behind it. Your improvement is an indicator that you are capable of leveraging the power of positive thinking and that neuroplasticity is working for you.

Finally, wherever you put a low number, journal about how this might be hurting your goals. Then go back to the practices you learned in this book that help you foster that positivity skill and brainstorm how you can include them in your implementation plan for achieving your goal. Putting direct focus on these specific skills will help you improve quickly.

POSITIVITY IN PRACTICE

I hope you feel nourished by knowing that you are worthy and capable of the self-care required to stay on the path to positivity. Not only is this an uplifting realization, but it's also the only way to succeed in anything meaningful. A flower cannot blossom without water, soil, and sunlight; similarly, you'll only be able to achieve the fullest expression of your goals and values when you cultivate the support and inner kindness you require to thrive. And based on the positivity assessment, you know where you'd like to grow even more. In order to achieve all the important goals you're working toward, how can you support yourself with self-care? What changes can you make in your life, relationships, and self-talk to allow yourself be forever flourishing?

CONCLUSION

There's an oft-told story about a British golf course in Calcutta during the British colonization of India. The British were expecting a relaxing golf experience like the ones played back home, but there was one huge obstacle they didn't anticipate: monkeys. The primates wouldn't let the British play in peace; wherever the ball was hit, they'd seize it, play with it, and toss it around. The golfers did everything in their power to control the monkeys: they built fences around the fairways, tried luring the monkeys away, and even attempted trapping the monkeys in cages. But nothing worked. For every monkey they managed, another would appear. Finally, the golfers accepted their reality and created a new rule: Play the ball where the monkey drops it.

When you're committed to positivity, your life is like a golf game on this Calcutta course. You studied the course, and you decided how you want to hit the ball in order to reach the holes; in other words, you consciously selected the positive thoughts, emotions, and behaviors you'll practice in order to make mean-ingful progress toward your goals. And yet, even when you take a perfect swing, monkeys can interrupt your hole-in-one and throw the ball in the sand. You can work hard for a promotion and then the economy can go into a recession. Or you might lose someone you love and be so overcome by grief that you feel like you have no control of your mind at all. These circumstances are challenging, frustrating, and even unfair, but that doesn't mean that you're doing a bad job or that you should quit. You just have to play the ball where the monkey drops it: Accept the circumstances as they are and continue playing for the love of the game—for the love of your own precious life. Positive thinking and living in alignment with your values makes the game itself fulfilling, so you're not reliant on perfect results, anyway.

When you *do* hit a line drive, or when the monkeys give you a lucky toss, remember to savor these experiences. Face it, feed it, and feel it! Bask in good thoughts and good times, as you would bask in the sunshine on the first day of summer. Remember, our need for survival has programmed each one of us with a negativity bias, where we're constantly scanning for what's wrong rather than what's right. You can, and will, overcome that bias by leaning into the little wins along the way. Maybe you were able to feel grateful for your life, even when you were sick in bed with the flu, or maybe you scored your first client yesterday. Actively celebrating and enriching these positive experiences not only makes them more enjoyable, it also helps create memories and resources that serve you throughout your whole life. Moreover, when you revel in making progress in something meaningful, you fill up your motivation tank to continue moving forward.

When the monkey throws your ball the wrong way, remember that the first step to getting back on track is simply pausing to examine the course and accept your current circumstances. Sometimes it may even feel like the monkey's inside your mind, and despite your best efforts at optimism, you'll feel unsettled, scared, or overwhelmed. Don't avoid or resist these negative thoughts; turn toward them with openness and kindness. As Martin Luther King, Jr., once said, "Love is the only force capable of transforming an enemy into a friend." When you pause to practice PAIN and self-compassion, these negative experiences transform into opportunities for self-awareness and self-care. Sitting face-to-face with your failure, fear, and sadness also proves that even if you are not feeling happy in every moment, you can always be courageous and caring. And that, as you've learned by now, is what positive thinking is really all about.

Make sure you have the systems in place to help you thrive. If you know where the hole is and you have a plan for how to hit your ball in that direction, you'll get there eventually, no matter how many times the mischievous monkeys get in the way. Similarly, if you're determined enough to reach your goals, and you stay committed to your intentions, you can trust that you'll always be moving in the right direction and that you don't have to force things. Moreover, if you're golfing with good people, laughing at your gaffs together, and supporting each other along the way, then it won't really matter how fast you finish the game, because you'll be delighting in each swing so much. This is why maintaining strong boundaries and sharing with a supportive community are critical components of cultivating positive progress.

Last, remember, there are no "shoulds" on this path. Positive thinking is about self-creation; what self you want to create is up to you. Let your values lead the way, and then tap into your Wise Mind whenever you need to make big decisions about the right way forward. Honoring your inner compass, over and over, is the best self-care practice I know.

You've reached the end of this book; but the truth is that this is just a beginning. You know where you want to go from here, and now you have the tools to make it happen. Keep measuring your progress as you move forward, as this will help you see your next steps clearly. And, most important, never forget how powerful you are. Every deep breath, every consciously created thought, every choice you make to try again after failure, every positive emotion you share with another person is evidence that you are capable of creating a positive life. The path to positivity is yours, my courageous reader. You just need to be willing to follow the twists and turns, ask for directions when you need help, and make a commitment to never turning back. Your life is worth it.

RESOURCES

BOOKS AND JOURNALS

Brach, Tara. *Radical Acceptance: Embracing Your Life with the Heart of a Buddha*. New York, NY: Bantam Dell, 2004.

Dobelli, Rolf. *The Art of Thinking Clearly*. London, United Kingdom: Sceptre, 2014.

Dweck, Carol. *Mindset: The New Psychology of Success: How We Can Learn to Fulfill Our Potential.* New York, NY: Ballantine, 2007.

Frankl, Victor. *Man's Search for Meaning*. Boston, MA: Beacon Press, 2006.

Fredrickson, Barbara. *Positivity*. New York, NY: Harmony Books, 2009.

Hanson, Rick. *Hardwiring Happiness: The New Brain Science of Contentment, Calm, and Confidence*. New York, NY: Harmony Books, 2016.

Jones, Gregory Knox. *Play the Ball Where the Monkey Drops It: Why We Suffer and How We Can Hope*. San Francisco, CA: Harper, 2001.

Kahneman, Daniel. *Thinking, Fast and Slow*. New York, NY: Farrar, Straus and Giroux, 2011.

Neff, Kristin. *Self-Compassion: The Proven Power of Being Kind to Yourself*. New York, NY: William Morrow, 2015.

Peterson, C. *Pursuing the Good Life: 100 Reflections on Positive Psychology*. New York, NY: Oxford University Press, 2012.

Seligman, M. *Authentic Happiness: Using the New Positive Psychology to Realize Your Potential for Lasting Fulfillment.* New York, NY: Free Press, 2002.

Taormina, Robert J., and Jennifer Hong Gao. "Maslow and the Motivation Hierarchy: Measuring Satisfaction of the Needs." *The American Journal of Psychology* 126, no. 2 (2013): 155. doi:10.5406/amerjpsyc.126.2.0155.

WEBSITES

Positive Psychology Community: https://positivepsychology.com/

Radiant Wholeness Holistic Life Coaching: www.caitlinmargaret.com

University of Pennsylvania's Positive Psychology Center: https://ppc.sas.upenn.edu/

PROGRAMS

Foundations of Well-Being: https://www.thefoundationsofwellbeing.com/

Freedom from Anxiety: http://www.caitlinmargaret.com/ffa/

Mindfulness-Based Stress Reduction: https://palousemindfulness.com/

The Mindful Self-Compassion Program: https://self-compassion.org/the-program/

The Science of Happiness: https://www.edx.org/course/the-science-of-happiness-4

GUIDED MEDITATIONS

Caitlin Margaret's Free Guided Meditations:
www.caitlinmargaret.com/pathtopositivity

Kristen Neff's Guided Self-Compassion Meditations:
https://self-compassion.org/guided-self-compassion
-meditations-mp3-2/

Mindfulness Meditations:
https://www.mindful.org/category/meditation/guided-meditation/

REFERENCES

Akhtar, Salman. "Patience." *Silent Virtues: Patience, Curiosity, Privacy, Intimacy, Humility, and Dignity.* New York, NY: Routledge, 2018.

Benson, Kyle. "The Magic Relationship Ratio, According to Science." The Gottman Institute. Accessed September 11, 2019. https://www.gottman.com/blog/the-magic-relationship-ratio -according-science/.

Blankert, Tim, and Melvyn R. W. Hamstra. "Imagining Success: Multiple Achievement Goals and the Effectiveness of Imagery." *Basic and Applied Social Psychology* 39, no. 1 (July 2016): 60–67. doi:10.1080/ 01973533.2016.1255947.

Brach, Tara. *Radical Acceptance: Embracing Your Life with the Heart of a Buddha.* New York, NY: Bantam Dell, 2004.

Brans, Karen, and Philippe Verduyn. "Intensity and Duration of Negative Emotions: Comparing the Role of Appraisals and Regulation Strategies." *PLoS ONE* 9, no. 3 (2014). doi:10.1371/journal. pone.0092410.

Brown, Brené. *The Gifts of Imperfection: Let Go of Who You Think You're Supposed to Be and Embrace Who You Are.* Center City, MN: Hazelden Publishing, 2010.

Buckingham, Marcus. *Now, Discover Your Strengths.* Gallup Press: Washington D.C., 2001.

Burns, David. *Feeling Good: The New Mood Therapy.* New York, NY: Signet, 1980.

Cameron, Kim, Carlos Mora, Trevor Leutscher, and Margaret Calarco. "Effects of Positive Practices on Organizational Effectiveness." *The*

Journal of Applied Behavioral Science 47, no. 3 (2011): 266–308. doi:10.1177/0021886310395514.

Caprara, Gian Vittorio, Bernadette Paula Luengo Kanacri, Antonio Zuffianò, Maria Gerbino, and Concetta Pastorelli. "Why and How to Promote Adolescents' Prosocial Behaviors: Direct, Mediated and Moderated Effects of the CEPIDEA School-Based Program." *Journal of Youth and Adolescence* 44, no. 12 (December 2015): 2211–29. doi:10.1007/s10964-015-0293-1.

Chattu, Vijayk, Banit Aeri, and Preeti Khanna. "Nutritional Aspects of Depression in Adolescents—A Systematic Review." *International Journal of Preventive Medicine* 10, no. 1 (2019): 42. doi:10.4103/ ijpvm.ijpvm_400_18.

Chevalier, Gaétan. "The Effect of Grounding the Human Body on Mood." *Psychological Reports* 116, no. 2 (2015): 534–42. doi:10.2466/06.pr0.116k21w5.

Clear, James. *Atomic Habits: Tiny Changes, Remarkable Results: An Easy & Proven Way to Build Good Habits & Break Bad Ones.* New York, NY: Avery, 2018.

Cohen, Geoffrey, and David Sherman. "The Psychology of Change: Self-Affirmation and Social Psychological Intervention." *Annual Review of Psychology* 65 (2014): 333 – 71. doi:10.1146/ annurev-psych-010213-115137.

Cox, Louis. "Overcoming Learning Aversion in Evaluating and Managing Uncertain Risks." *Risk Analysis* 35 (2015): 1892 – 1910. doi:10.1111/risa.12511.

Crane, Frederick G., and Erinn Crane. "Dispositional Optimism and Entrepreneurial Success." *The Psychologist-Manager Journal* 10, no. 1 (2007): 13 – 25. doi:10.1080/10887150709336610.

Day, Liz, Katie Hanson, John Maltby, Carmel Proctor, and Alex Wood. "Hope Uniquely Predicts Objective Academic Achievement above Intelligence, Personality, and Previous Academic Achievement." *Journal of Research in Personality* 44, no. 4 (2010): 550–53. doi:10.1016/j.jrp.2010.05.009.

Dobelli, Rolf. *The Art of Thinking Clearly*. London, United Kingdom: Sceptre, 2014.

Dockray, Samantha, and Andrew Steptoe. (2010). "Positive Affect and Psychobiological Processes." *Neuroscience and Biobehavioral Reviews* 35 (2019): 69 - 75. doi:10.1016/j.neubiorev.2010.01.006.

Dweck, Carol. *Mindset: Changing the Way You Think to Fulfil Your Potential*. New York, NY: Robinson, 2017.

Egan, Sarah, Tracey Wade, Roz Shafran, and Martin Antony. *Cognitive-Behavioral Treatment of Perfectionism*. New York, NY: Guilford, 2014.

Feeney, Brooke, and Nancy Collins. "A New Look at Social Support: An Integrative Perspective on Thriving through Relationships." *Personality and Social Psychology Review,* (2014): 1 - 35. doi: 10.1177/1088868314544222.

Flett, Gordon, Paul Hewitt, Kirk Blankstein, and Lisa Gray. "Psychological Distress and the Frequency of Perfectionistic Thinking." *Journal of Personality and Social Psychology* 75, no. 5 (1998): 1363 - 81. doi:10.1037/0022-3514.75.5.1363.

Fredrickson, Barbara. "The Broaden-and-Build Theory of Positive Emotions." *Philosophical Transactions of the Royal Society of London B Biological Sciences* 359, no. 1149 (2004): 1367 - 78. doi: 10.1098/rstb.2004.1512.

Fox, Kieran, Evan Thompson, Jessica R. Andrews-Hanna, and Kalina Christoff. "Is Thinking Really Aversive? A Commentary on Wilson Et Al.s 'Just Think: The Challenges of a Disengaged Mind.'" *Frontiers in Psychology*, Last modified July 2, 2018. doi:10.31231/osf.io/murj3.

Germer, Christopher K., and Kristin D. Neff. "Self-Compassion in Clinical Practice." *Journal of Clinical Psychology* 69, no. 8 (2013): 856–67. doi:10.1002/jclp.22021.

Gilbert, Daniel Todd. *Stumbling on Happiness*. New York, NY: Vintage, 2007.

Goleman, Daniel, and Richard J. Davidson. *Altered Traits: Science Reveals How Meditation Changes Your Mind, Brain, and Body*. New York, NY: Avery, 2018.

Gollwitzer, Peter M., and Paschal Sheeran. "Implementation Intentions and Goal Achievement: A Meta-Analysis of Effects and Processes." *Advances in Experimental Social Psychology Advances in Experimental Social Psychology, 38* (2006): 69–119. doi:10.1016/s0065-2601(06)38002-1.

Gordon, Brett R., Mark Lyons, and Matthew P. Herring. "The Effect of Resistance Exercise Training on Anxiety Symptoms." *Medicine & Science in Sports & Exercise* 49 (2017): 471. doi:10.1249/01.mss.0000518180.45240.a8.

Gottman, John Mordechai. *What Predicts Divorce? The Measures*. Mahwah, NJ: Lawrence Erlbaum Associates, 1996.

Greenberg, Melanie. *The Stress-Proof Brain: Master Your Emotional Response to Stress Using Mindfulness & Neuroplasticity*. Strawberry Hills, New South Wales: ReadHowYouWant, 2018.

Grossmann, Igor, Baljinder Sahdra, and Ciarrochi, Joseph. "A Heart and A Mind: Self-Distancing Facilitates the Association Between Heart Rate Variability, and Wise Reasoning." *Frontiers in Behavioral Neuroscience* 10 (2016): 1 - 10. doi:10.3389/fnbeh.2016.00068.

Hall, Jeffrey A. "How Many Hours Does It Take to Make a Friend?" *Journal of Social and Personal Relationships* 36, no. 4 (2018): 1278–96. doi:10.1177/0265407518761225.

Hanson, Rick. *Hardwiring Happiness: The New Brain Science of Contentment, Calm, and Confidence*. New York, NY: Harmony Books, 2016.

Harris, Peter R., Dale W. Griffin, Lucy E. Napper, Rod Bond, Benjamin Schüz, Christopher Stride, and Irina Brearley. "Individual Differences in Self-Affirmation: Distinguishing Self-Affirmation from Positive Self-Regard." *Self and Identity* 18, no. 6 (2018): 589–630. doi:10.1080/15298868.2018.1504819.

Harris, Russ, and Stephen Hayes. *The Happiness Trap*. London, United Kingdom: Robinson, 2008.

Harvard Health Publishing. "Why It's Hard to Change Unhealthy Behavior—and Why You Should Keep Trying." *Harvard Health*. Accessed July 15, 2019. https://www.health.harvard.edu/news-letter_article/why-its-hard-to-change-unhealthy-behavior-and-why-you-should-keep-trying.

Hattie, John, and Helen Timperley. "The Power of Feedback." *Review of Educational Research* 77, no. 1 (2007): 81–112. doi:10.3102/003465430298487.

Hirsch, Colette R., Gemma Perman, Sarra Hayes, Claire Eagleson, and Andrew Mathews. "Delineating the Role of Negative Verbal Thinking in Promoting Worry, Perceived Threat, and Anxiety." *Clinical Psychological Science* 3, no. 4 (June 2015): 637–47. doi:10.1177/2167702615577349.

Hjemdal, Odin, Tore Stiles, and Adrian Wells. "Automatic Thoughts and Meta-Cognition as Predictors of Depressive or Anxious Symptoms: A Prospective Study of Two Trajectories." *Scandinavian Journal of Psychology* 54, no. 2 (2012): 59–65. https://doi.org/10.1111/sjop.12010.

Hofmann, Stefan G., and Angelina F. Gómez. "Mindfulness-Based Interventions for Anxiety and Depression." *Psychiatric Clinics of North America* 40, no. 4 (2017): 739–49. doi:10.1016/j.psc.2017.08.008.

Ito, Tiffany A., Jeff T. Larsen, N. Kyle Smith, and John T. Cacioppo. "Negative Information Weighs More Heavily on the Brain: The Negativity Bias in Evaluative Categorizations." *Journal of Personality and Social Psychology* 75, no. 4 (1998): 887–900. doi:10.1037//0022-3514.75.4.887.

James, Kirsty, and Katharine A. Rimes. "Mindfulness-Based Cognitive Therapy Versus Pure Cognitive Behavioural Self-Help for Perfectionism: A Pilot Randomised Study." *Mindfulness* 9, no. 3 (2017): 801–14. doi:10.1007/s12671-017-0817-8.

Khawaja, Nigar, and Lai Ngo Heidi Yu. "A Comparison of the 27-Item and 12-Item Intolerance of Uncertainty Scales." *Clinical Psychologist* 14, no. 3 (2010): 97–106. doi:10.1080/13284207.2010.502542.

Kim, Eun Seong, Yeon-Ju Hong, Minwoo Kim, Eun Joo Kim, and Jae-Jin Kim. "Relationship Between Self-Esteem and Self-Consciousness in Adolescents: An Eye-Tracking Study." *Psychiatry Investigation* 16, no. 4 (2019): 306–13. doi:10.30773/pi.2019.02.10.3.

Klenger, F. "Exercise as a Treatment for Depression: A Meta-Analysis Adjusting for Publication Bias." *Physioscience* 12, no. 03 (September 2016): 122–23. doi:10.1055/s-0035-1567129.

Kline, Daniel B. "A Majority of U.S. Workers Are Actually Satisfied with Their Jobs." *USA Today*. Gannett Satellite Information Network. September 7, 2018. https://www.usatoday.com/story/money/careers/employment-trends/2018/09/03/labor-day-majority-workers-satisfied-jobs-survey/37670201/.

Ladouceur, Robert, Patrick Gosselin, and Michel J Dugas. "Experimental Manipulation of Intolerance of Uncertainty: A Study of a Theoretical Model of Worry." *Behaviour Research and Therapy* 38, no. 9 (2000): 933–41. doi:10.1016/s0005-7967(99)00133-3.

Lazarus, Richard S., and Susan Folkman. *Stress, Appraisal, and Coping*. New York, NY: Springer, 1984.

Linehan, Marsha. *Skills Training Manual for Treating Borderline Personality Disorder*. New York, NY: Guilford Press, 1993.

Lin-Siegler, Xiaodong, Janet N. Ahn, Jondou Chen, Fu-Fen Anny Fang, and Myra Luna-Lucero. "Even Einstein Struggled: Effects of Learning about Great Scientists' Struggles on High School Students' Motivation to Learn Science." *Journal of Educational Psychology* 108, no. 3 (2016): 314–28. doi:10.1037/edu0000092.

Lyubomirsky, Sonja, Laura King, and Ed Diener. "The Benefits of Frequent Positive Affect: Does Happiness Lead to Success?" *Psychological Bulletin* 131, no. 6 (2005): 803–55. doi:10.1037/0033-2909.131.6.803.

Magnuson, Cale D., and Lynn A. Barnett. "The Playful Advantage: How Playfulness Enhances Coping with Stress." *Leisure Sciences* 35, no. 2 (2013): 129–44. doi:10.1080/01490400.2013.761905.

Mak, Winnie W. S., Ivy S. W. Ng, and Celia C. Y. Wong. "Resilience: Enhancing Well-Being Through the Positive Cognitive Triad." *Journal of Counseling Psychology* 58, no. 4 (2011): 610–17. doi:10.1037/a0025195.

Manzoni, Gian Mauro, Francesco Pagnini, Gianluca Castelnuovo, and Enrico Molinari. "Relaxation Training for Anxiety: A Ten-Years Systematic Review with Meta-Analysis." *BMC Psychiatry* 8, no. 1 (February 2008). doi:10.2147/oajct.s6464510.1186/1471-244x-8-41.

Mauss, Iris B., Maya Tamir, Craig L. Anderson, and Nicole S. Savino. "Can Seeking Happiness Make People Unhappy? Paradoxical Effects of Valuing Happiness." *Emotion* 11, no. 4 (2011): 807–15. doi:10.1037/a0022010.

Meeten, F., S. R. Dash, A. L. S. Scarlet, and G. C. L. Davey. "Investigating the Effect of Intolerance of Uncertainty on Catastrophic Worrying and Mood." *Behaviour Research and Therapy* 50, no. 11 (2012): 690–98. doi:10.1016/j.brat.2012.08.003.

Milne, Sarah, Sheina Orbell, and Paschal Sheeran. "Combining Motivational and Volitional Interventions to Promote Exercise Participation: Protection Motivation Theory and Implementation Intentions." *British Journal of Health Psychology* 7, no. 2 (2002): 163–84. doi:10.1348/135910702169420.

Moskowitz, Judy, Adam Carrico, Michael Cohn, Larissa G. Duncan, Cori Bussolari, Kristin Layous, Jen Hult, et al. "Randomized Controlled Trial of a Positive Affect Intervention to Reduce Stress in People Newly Diagnosed with HIV; Protocol and Design for the IRISS Study." *Open Access Journal of Clinical Trials* 2014, 85. doi:10.2147/oajct.s64645.

"Most Americans Experience Feeling Dissatisfied with How Their Body Looks from Time to Time, Including Nearly Two in Five Who Feel This Way Whenever They Look in the Mirror." *Ipsos*. Accessed September 9, 2019. https://www.ipsos.com/en-us/news-polls/most-americans-experience-feeling-dissatisfied-with-body-looks-from-time-to-time.

Myrskylä, Mikko, and Rachel Margolis. "Happiness: Before and After the Kids." *Demography* 51, no. 5 (2014): 1843–66. doi:10.1007/s13524-014-0321-x.

Neff, Kristin. *Self-Compassion: Stop Beating Yourself Up and Leave Insecurity Behind*. New York, NY: William Morrow, 2015.

Neff, Kristin D., Kristin L. Kirkpatrick, and Stephanie S. Rude. "Self-Compassion and Adaptive Psychological Functioning." *Journal of Research in Personality* 41, no. 1 (2007): 139–54. doi:10.1016/j.jrp.2006.03.004.

"New Cigna Study Reveals Loneliness at Epidemic Levels in America." Cigna, a Global Health Insurance and Health Service Company. Accessed July 21, 2019. https://www.cigna.com/newsroom/news-releases/2018/new-cigna-study-reveals-loneliness-at-epidemic-levels-in-america.

O'Connell, Brenda H., Deirdre O'Shea, and Stephen Gallagher. "Enhancing Social Relationships Through Positive Psychology Activities: A Randomised Controlled Trial." *The Journal of Positive Psychology* 11, no. 2 (June 2015): 149–62. doi:10.1080/17439760.2015.1037860.

O'Neil, Adrienne, Michael Berk, Catherine Itsiopoulos, David Castle, Rachelle Opie, Josephine Pizzinga, Laima Brazionis, et al. "A Randomised, Controlled Trial of a Dietary Intervention for Adults with Major Depression (the 'SMILES' Trial): Study Protocol." *BMC Psychiatry* 13, no. 1 (2013). doi:10.1186/1471-244x-13-114.

Ong, Anthony D., C. S. Bergeman, Toni L. Bisconti, and Kimberly A. Wallace. "Psychological Resilience, Positive Emotions, and Successful Adaptation to Stress in Later Life." *Journal of Personality and Social Psychology* 91, no. 4 (2006): 730–49. doi:10.1037/0022-3514.91.4.730.

Otake, Keiko, Satoshi Shimai, Junko Tanaka-Matsumi, Kanako Otsui, and Barbara L. Fredrickson. "Happy People Become Happier Through Kindness: A Counting Kindnesses Intervention." *Journal of Happiness Studies* 7, no. 3 (2006): 361–75. doi:10.1007/s10902-005-3650-z.

Park, Nansook, Christopher Peterson, Daniel Szvarca, Randy J. Vander Molen, Eric S. Kim, Kevin Collon. "Positive Psychology and Physical Health." *American Journal of Lifestyle Medicine* 10, no. 3 (2016). doi:10.1177/1559827614550277.

Pascual-Leone, A., D. Nguyet, L. G. Cohen, J. P. Brasil-Neto, A. Cammarota, and M. Hallett. "Modulation of Muscle Responses Evoked by Transcranial Magnetic Stimulation during the Acquisition of New Fine Motor Skills." *Journal of Neurophysiology* 74, no. 3 (January 1995): 1037–45. doi:10.1152/jn.1995.74.3.1037.

Pink, Daniel H. *Drive: The Surprising Truth About What Motivates Us.* Edinburgh, Scotland: Canongate Books, 2018.

Rygula, Rafal, Joanna Golebiowska, Jakub Kregiel, Jakub Kubik, and Piotr Popik. "Effects of Optimism on Motivation in Rats." *Frontiers in Behavioral Neuroscience* 9 (2015). doi:10.3389/fnbeh.2015.00032.

Santos, Veruska, Flavia Paes, Valeska Pereira, Oscar Arias-Carrión, Adriana Cardoso Silva, Mauro Giovanni Carta, Antonio Egidio Nardi, and Sergio Machado. "The Role of Positive Emotion and Contributions of Positive Psychology in Depression Treatment: Systematic Review." *Clinical Practice & Epidemiology in Mental Health* 9, no. 1 (2013): 221–37. doi:10.2174/1745017901309010221.

Schuch, Felipe B., Davy Vancampfort, Justin Richards, Simon Rosenbaum, Philip B. Ward, and Brendon Stubbs. "Exercise as a Treatment for Depression: A Meta-Analysis Adjusting for Publication Bias." *Journal of Psychiatric Research* 77 (2016): 42–51. doi:10.1016/j.jpsychires.2016.02.023.

Scotland-Coogan, Diane, and Erin Davis. "Relaxation Techniques for Trauma." *Journal of Evidence-Informed Social Work* 13, no. 5 (2016): 434–41. doi:10.1080/23761407.2016.1166845.

Seligman, Martin E. P., Tracy A. Steen, Nansook Park, and Christopher Peterson. "Positive Psychology Progress: Empirical Validation of Interventions." *American Psychologist* 60, no. 5 (2005): 410–21. doi:10.1037/0003-066x.60.5.410.

Shafran, Roz, Sarah Egan, and Tracey Wade. *Overcoming Perfectionism: A Self-Help Guide Using Scientifically Supported Cognitive Behavioural Techniques*. London, United Kingdom: Robinson, 2018.

Sirgy, M. Joseph, and Jiyun Wu. "The Pleasant Life, the Engaged Life, and the Meaningful Life: What About the Balanced Life?" *Happiness Studies Book Series: The Exploration of Happiness* (2013): 175–91. doi:10.1007/978-94-007-5702-8_10.

Somov, Pavel G. *Present Perfect: A Mindfulness Approach to Letting Go of Perfectionism and the Need for Control*. Oakland, CA: New Harbinger Publications, 2010.

Srivastava, Sanjay, Kelly M. McGonigal, Jane M. Richards, Emily A. Butler, and James Gross. 2019. "Optimism in Close Relationships: How Seeing Things in a Positive Light Makes Them So." *Journal of Personality and Social Psychology 91, no. 1 (2006): 143–53* doi:10.1037/0022-3514.91.1.143.

Tay, Louis, and Ed Diener. "Needs and Subjective Well-Being Around the World." *Journal of Personality and Social Psychology* 101, no. 2 (2011): 354–65. doi:10.1037/a0023779.

Toepfer, Steven, and Kathleen Walker. "Letters of Gratitude: Improving Well-Being Through Expressive Writing." *Journal of Writing Research* 1, no. 3 (2009): 181–98. doi:10.17239/jowr-2009.01.03.1.

Tolin, David F. "Is Cognitive–Behavioral Therapy More Effective Than Other Therapies? A Meta-Analytic Review." *Clinical Psychology Review* 30, no. 6 (2010): 710–20. doi:10.1016/j.cpr.2010.05.003.

Van Diest, Ilse, Karen Verstappen, André E. Aubert, Devy Widjaja, Debora Vansteenwegen, and Elke Vlemincx. "Inhalation/Exhalation Ratio Modulates the Effect of Slow Breathing on Heart Rate Variability and Relaxation." *Applied Psychophysiology and Biofeedback* 39, no. 3–4 (2014): 171–80. doi:10.1007/s10484-014-9253-x.

Waldinger, Robert. "What Makes a Good Life? Lessons from the Longest Study on Happiness." Filmed November 2015 in Boston, MA. TED video, 12:47. https://www.ted.com/talks/robert_waldinger_what_makes_a_good_life_lessons_from_the_longest_study_on_happiness/up-next?language=en.

Watkins, Philip C., and Duncan McCurrach. "Progress in the Science of Gratitude." *The Oxford Handbook of Positive Psychology,* 3rd Edition, June 2017. doi:10.1093/oxfordhb/9780199396511.013.33.

Whitehead, Nadia, "People Would Rather Be Electrically Shocked Than Left Alone With Their Thoughts." *Science*, December 10, 2017. www.sciencemag.org/news/2014/07/people-would-rather-be-electrically-shocked-left-alone-their-thoughts.

INDEX

ACKNOWLEDGMENTS

I am overwhelmed with gratitude toward the teachers who guided me along my own path to positivity, including those with whom I studied directly, Tara Brach, Rick Hanson, Sally Kempton, and those whose teachings I closely follow, Byron Katie and Brené Brown. Without your wisdom, I can't imagine where I would be today. It's your insight that shines through these pages, and I am humbled to be a part of the movements you lead. And to my other greatest teachers, the indigenous communities in Guatemala, Rwanda, and India that I had the privilege of working with, who embody—amidst the most challenging circumstances—what positivity, resiliency, and love are all about.

I'm also thankful to the team at Callisto Media, especially my editor Nora Spiegel, without whom this book would not exist. And to all those who breathe life into my personal adventures: to my mother, who tirelessly said yes to my dreams when everyone else said "you want to do what?!" and who passed down her brilliant ways with the pen; to my father, for the playful childhood adventures that still fill me with positivity today, and for teaching me how to teach; to my beloved husband and in-laws, who are an endless source of laughter and light in my life; to my friends, mentors, and siblings, who positively encouraged me when I needed it the most, especially Sara, Rachel, Liz, Iza, Paco, Chrissy, Natasha, and Sanjeev; and of course, to Mahashakti and Pachamama, for the delicious grace of every sweet breath.

And, lastly, I'm extremely grateful for the people I have had the good fortune to coach, for helping create a more positive world through your courageous transformations.

ABOUT THE AUTHOR

Caitlin Margaret is the founder of Radiant Wholeness, a holistic coaching practice that supports soul-centered people to navigate crises, connect and express their authentic self, build wellness, and create purposeful work. She received her MS in social work from Columbia University in 2011, and she has over a decade of training from global institutions in positive psychology, mindfulness, functional nutrition, and integrative wellness. Before she started coaching, Caitlin lived in Latin America for two years and in India for five years, where she helped launch and scale several high-impact social enterprises.